AF252000

GOD DOES NOT FEED THE BIRDS...
I Do

LAURA FIORENTINO

Aster Press
an imprint of Blue Fortune Enterprises LLC

GOD DOES NOT FEED THE BIRDS… I DO
Copyright © 2021 by Laura Fiorentino.

All rights reserved. Printed in the United States of America. No part of this book may be used or reproduced in any manner whatsoever without written permission except in the case of brief quotations embodied in critical articles or reviews.

Thank you for buying an authorized edition of this book and for complying with copyright laws by not reproducing, scanning or distributing any portion of the contents without written permission.

This story, experiences and words are the author's.

For information contact :
Blue Fortune Enterprises, LLC
Aster Press
P.O. Box 554
Yorktown, VA 23690
http://blue-fortune.com

Book and Cover design by Gretchen Bedell, Odd Moxie
Edited by Jane Handa

ISBN: 978-1-948979-58-0
First Edition: February 2021

Dedication

This piece of writing is dedicated to Ernest Hemingway who taught me to "write hard and clear about what hurts."

For Daddy.

1
Signposts

"I love you, son. Call me if you need anything. I promise not to bother you and please don't let your father drive." I hold my youngest in my arms, wondering how he has coped with our mounting marital issues and the transition to college. The pickup is packed with all his material needs, but I can't be certain I've prepared him well for his emotional ones. I whisper in his ear, "I'm sorry," while his father carries a six pack, minus the two beers he's already consumed, by its yoke to the truck. I wince inside, and there is that familiar *why the hell is this always the way* feeling, too. "Let's go," he says, and my son and I release our embrace, and my countenance reveals my heart's ache. "What's your problem?" His words cut me down, and I lower my head. As they drive off, I ask my son to forgive my cowardice and inability to confront his father's disrespect toward me and irresponsible behavior toward him.

Later that day, as I sit on a bench at the learning garden, I stew behind a pair of Ray-Bans. It is August and unseasonably chilly. I grab a sweatshirt on my way out, but it is not enough to temper the cold front pushing its way through Poquoson. A mist is along for the ride; it obscures my view like a lace curtain, and I smell rain in the air. At least it is not too humid, only 75 percent, which really isn't bad for southern Virginia during the summer. Off to the left is a native echinacea in bloom. She is tall and her stems give with the wind, back and forth, back and forth. Her hypnotic effect momentarily assuages the angst within me. To the right is Helianthus giganticus, the name a kindred soul and I gave to this late summer blooming sunflower like plant that tickles the clouds with her daisy-like petals. The wind has no impact on this staunch beauty; she stands tall, unwavering, confident. Between the two is the path to the garden which has an array of perennials, annuals, herbs and bushes on either side of it.

Standing at its threshold, the metaphor does not go unnoticed. My marriage is this path: straight, flat, predictable, with clearly defined boundaries. My faith in the notion that it is greater than us and purposeful has sustained me. It will not go unrewarded in this life because God loves me and has a plan. Yet, I am struggling and pondering. Have I been mistaken? Maybe there is no "reward" here; maybe God has other plans. The garden path wants me to follow it, and I do, but I hesitate for a moment, knowing it will pressure me to look beyond the flora to what has been, and I have an inkling it is not Primrose Lane.

We had known each other for two years before we married but only spent ten weeks together. We filled the space between us with letters. I remember the "fams," and I remember how much he enjoyed flying the T34, especially when he learned to do rolls and loops. His words leaped off the pages of those letters. I was happy to focus on him and my graduate studies. Our separation was tolerable because it is enough to read the words "I love you"; "I trust you"; and "I know you'll be faithful." Our situation was irresistibly romantic as well; he was in flight school, and I was in Boston longing and waiting patiently for him and our life to begin.

With a verdant imagination, I created our marriage; though not grand, it is safe, comfortable and filled with love. It did not matter where we went or how we lived. I craved closeness and wanted to be valued. He made his desires clear.

"Will you cook for me?"

"Yes."

"And the house?"

"I'll take care of you."

I juggled graduate school and wedding plans. *Wedding... wedding?* My train of thought abruptly pauses, and I notice the Russian sage is spindly and toppling over into Lantana, which is in full bloom. The blue-purple and yellow look lovely together, and I think about France during the reign of Louis XVI. Those were among his favorite colors. *Wedding... wedding... wedding,* and then it hits me—his friend's wedding in New Jersey we attended while engaged. The train moves on.

He never explained why he subjected me to his drunken, disorderly behavior at their wedding. Spilling red wine on his dress whites and the floor, he staggered across the parquet following two young women he thought were dancing with him. Flirtatious and laughing, he tried to pick either one up. They quickened their pace as they looked to me. Humiliated, I turned away, got up and left the room.

I confronted him in our hotel room after the reception, but my words ricocheted off him, the walls and back to me. I threw him off the bed; he bounced back onto it. I propped myself on the club chair next to the window, unsure if the cold sprinting up my spine came from the air conditioning unit. The next morning, he dropped me at the airport in Newark, no explanation, no goodbye, no hug, no kiss. Worse, I was not sure he remembered anything, and I dared not ask. "See ya," he said before walking away.

I scribbled words on lined paper telling him I cannot marry someone who is discourteous, perhaps disingenuous and eager to drink whenever the occasion arises. I mailed the missive hastily while I had the courage but almost immediately regretted doing so. Fear. Lying on Mother's bed with her and my sister, I thought out loud after his response comes.

"Did I do the right thing?"

My sister asked, "What did he say?"

"It won't happen again; I won't drink like that again; You matter more than anyone else; I love you."

"Wow," she said.

"He also says, I can't take it if you don't marry me."

"He made a mistake…"

"I don't know."

"It's your choice," Mother said.

A collection of words was all it took for me to chalk the episode up to "one of those things," and as a hopeless romantic in a dime store novel, I took him back, dismissing the event and advising myself that my reaction is over the top. We were young, and young people drink to have fun, right? So, I moved forward, trusting his words. After all, he was a Naval officer.

As an aviator, his exceptional intelligence and dexterity earned him honors with distinction in flight school, an impressive accomplishment considering the company he kept there. He flew me to Florida for graduation. I was nervous as I stood before his classmates and their loved ones on January 11, 1985 at NAS Whiting, in Milton, Florida. He stood straight, tall and still, his arms stationed at his sides, hands slightly cupped, attentive to HT-18's CO. Fourteen-carat gold wings were pinned to his chest with trembling hands just above his heart, and I pricked myself after I punctured his uniform with them. It was my engagement gift, engraved with his initials and graduation date.

"Look at this." He motioned me to lean over to the driver's seat. "I'm one of a thousand or more people who will be designated a naval aviator this year." He held a business card, white with an embossed set of gold wings and his name and aviator designation number in black. "This is my number." He placed his finger on it before underscoring it several times. "I am a naval aviator."

"Number one in your class too," I leaned over and kissed his cheek. "Who gave this to you?"

"The Command."

His graduation from flight school was my first act as his betrothed. I belonged to him, and after we celebrated at a local bar with his classmates, I returned to Boston and attended to graduate school and our wedding.

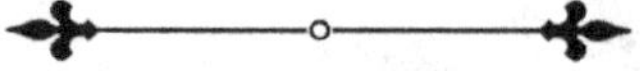

The seamstress tucks here and nips there; and as I watch her through the mirror, I cannot help but feel lonely. This event is meant to be shared with those who love me, but I am alone in a big room watching a stranger fit me for a dress that belongs to my mother. Don't get me wrong, it is glorious, one of a kind, tailored by seamstresses from the house of Bianci in Boston. It is covered with hand tatted lace and mother-of-pearl, and it has a five-foot train, but I am not smiling as my eyes scan the contours of my body, and I am not unhappy. I am somewhere else, lost in a story I am developing for a screen writing class about two sisters in an African country on the verge of civil war.

Both sisters are symbols: one traditional, one revolutionary. The protagonist, Jacinta, is me, the me I wish to be but cannot; she forges beyond the constraints of convention and clears the brush that prevents her from laying her own path. Her sister is fearful, and she is me too, the me I am, and this screenplay is my attempt to sort me out. Although I know the climax of the story, I am struggling with the rising action, building in enough suspense to accentuate the climax. Perhaps I need to go back and establish the sisters' relationship more poignantly? Maybe build in conflict that draws them near? It is hard to say, but I enjoy the challenge to sort it out, obviously hopeful that I will be sorted out too. When I cross my arms and rest my chin on my hand, the seamstress says, "Basta!" My arms return to their place. "Bene."

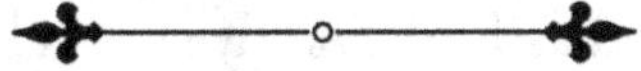

In the vestibule of St. Brigid for several minutes before I make the first step in what is to be a life of steps to him for better or worse, I find myself in another time, though in the same space. Shadows appear in the sanctuary all around me, dressed in black and gray. They fill the pews until they overflow, leaving many souls leaning against the walls, their heads bowed, some praying, some crying, all there to eulogize my father, to witness his transition to the next world. It is sixteen years ago, and it is real… again.

There I am, eight years old, at the front of the church to the right of the altar with my mother and siblings turned around on my knees and looking out at the people assembled. I was overwhelmed then, just trying to fathom the unfathomable. I am a young woman now and I have my faith to keep me balanced. I pause and contemplate the man who passed from this plane. I can never know who he was for myself, only through others' perceptions, which can be limited or skewed depending on their vision. What is clear is the collection of individuals from all walks of life and stations wait to say goodbye to their friend; and this is what he must have been above everything he achieved in forty-four years on this planet, a good friend, someone to trust and laugh with. I do remember his laugh; it was hearty. He opened his mouth wide and it looked as though he was saying, "Yay!" again and again. I call him Yayyay for this reason. Indeed, my father was a friend and confidant, and he is my daddy, and I have memories of life with him that come into view from time to time. They do not pass without note and sorrow. It is my wedding day and all of them join me in the vestibule, and I see them clearly, but there aren't that many. Our time together was short. I look to the altar and see my groom, and I promise my unborn children they will have a lifetime of memories; they will not miss that which I cannot define.

The music crescendos, it is my cue to begin the journey to my future. I choose to walk alone because no one can replace my beloved father, and with my head down, I struggle to cope with the tears and aches thoughts of him bring. Both are aroused by this milestone. From inside, I am summoned to look up, and as I do, Daddy shows himself to the right of the altar beneath a painting of Jesus and Joseph. He blesses me with a perfect love and fades away. My eye catches a dear friend whose beauty compels me to smile. I take my groom's arm before we kneel.

He wears dress whites, stands with near perfect posture, and embraces the first two fingers of his left hand before he fiddles with his academy ring on his right. It's uncomfortable there, and after three days pass, he puts it back on his ring finger. His wedding ring is relegated to a dresser drawer where it is forgotten. He sways, and I try to quell the butterflies flipping about within, rubbing my stomach until I feel conspicuous.

We are cognizant of the commitment we make, an irrevocable contract, a sacrament ordained by God, blessed by the priest and witnessed by our family. A gentle breeze comes in through the front doors of the church and keeps me cool. It is a gorgeous day in June, 70 degrees with little humidity… the perfect spring day; and for me, it represents the goodness of life and a sign that my marriage is blessed… meant to be, so it will be filled with good things, and he and I will devote ourselves to each other and our family. This is love. "I take you to be my husband, to love and cherish, from this day forward, in sickness and in health, in good times and bad, for as long as we both shall live." We light candles, receive the Eucharist, and seal the covenant with a kiss. Father says, "Molte benedizioni…tanti fiori mentrre vivi," roughly translated, "Many blessings be bestowed upon you and may your life be filled with flowers." A lovely thought that enlivens me as I walk up the aisle after Mass, picture our home and the beautiful garden I intend to plant. Many years passed before my wedding day garden came to fruition. Many of the plants in the learning garden are in my garden as well. These classic beauties perform for years and sow freely if they are happy. My intention is to be in this space and one with nature, to observe the birds, bees, and butterflies who know their place and how to live simply in alignment with their surroundings. I do envy them.

I hear the familiar *whop whop whop* sounds of a helicopter flying overhead, and before I look up, I discern which it might be, a habit I developed after years as a naval aviator's wife. I am not disappointed; I know it is she, the H53, dubbed by him "the flying pig." As she lumbers through the cloudy sky, her utterances remind me of our introduction thirty years prior when still a bride. I take a deep breath, and as I exhale, I fight the urge to revisit then; I'd much rather focus on this garden, take in its colors, textures, heights and depths and leave the past behind. Not possible, unfortunately, because I am not at peace, so I search for it in all the usual places past and present.

He is not home much during our first year together because he is scheduled to long cruise after the holidays. Throughout the fall, he prepares for the mission. This includes short cruises for two, four or six weeks at a time and sometimes longer workdays. He also has duty every now and again, and in my eagerness to be a good wife, I prepare dinner for him one Sunday night while he stands watch.

Charred burgers and over-salted dishes are routine. At one point, I take the battery out of the smoke detector that hangs in our kitchen. Chicken parmesan is an easy meal because the oven does most of the work. I prepare, bake, and then pack it in a picnic basket we received as a wedding gift, along with a salad and garlic bread.

I travel down 3rd Avenue on base, and what I don't know is this road has a crossing for helicopters that bridge the tarmac and their squadrons. There is a traffic light, but not a civilian one. It is a simple apparatus, a globe light fixture on top of a pole, and it is flashing red. I have no idea what it is signaling until the last minute when the "flying pig" comes out from my blind spot just before I am about to T-bone her.

I slam on the brakes. The hulking gal passes in front of me, no more than four feet away, oblivious, plugging along as though I am not there. The picnic basket is upside down on the floor in front on the passenger side; and I lunge for it, scooping it up and flipping it over. Sauce oozes through the cracks of the weave onto my hands and the clothes I wear. The adrenaline rush cripples me, so I sit in that spot for a good while. I gawk at her until she is out of sight.

When I finally meet him, he leads me to the officers' room where I set the basket on a table. I am shaking.

He looks me over. "What happened to you?"

"I almost hit that huge Marine helicopter!"

"The H53?"

"The pig one!"

"The 53."

"I didn't know there's a traffic light there! Who lets a helicopter cross a road?" I pace back and forth. "It's ruined—supper is ruined!"

"What did you do?"

"I didn't do anything."

"Did you see the light?"

"I saw it, but I didn't know what it meant."

He laughs. "It's there for a reason."

"I didn't know."

"Now you do."

My hands shake while I unpack. "The basket is ruined, ruined forever." The chicken, tossed salad and bread are in a heap. He picks through the mess and eats the chicken and a couple pieces of bread. My appetite is in the car.

It is as if it was preordained that she come into my world at this moment to remind me of the early years of our marriage. To what end, though? Is there something there to cling to, a common thread that holds us together through our present existence? Her rotors speak and I say, "I haven't thought of you in years." I expect a response from the flying heap of metal, but her voice dwindles to a mere murmur as she bulldozes her way out of sight. My attention is drawn back to the garden where the bright purple bracts of the Mexican sage bush on my right punctuate the surrounding mist, as though it is a lighthouse, and its white flowers are a beacon of light guiding me. Thinking about the H53 conjures up other memories, some not so bad. One quite nice, and I share it with you smiling.

I join the wives' club before he goes to sea, and I enjoy the companionship it offers. I attend meetings and social functions, experiencing graciousness and support from older women, particularly the CO's and XO's wives, Lois and Beth. My time with them is invaluable. Their entertaining anecdotes about service life teach me how to be a military wife.

I ask, "How long have you been doing this?"

Beth laughs. "We've hacked it for twelve years."

"How do you deal with homecomings?" My question arouses gentle laughter from Lois.

She quips, "You'll be okay, and here's what you do when you have children."

I lean in toward her.

"Go to the bank and buy many rolls of quarters, maybe five or six, maybe more, depending."

Beth playfully adds, "I think no more than seven."

Lois continues, "When you get home from the pier with your husband, unroll the coins, throw all the quarters out back and then turn your kids loose before you attend to him."

She looks at me, woman to woman, her eyes fixed on mine before her mighty laugh almost dismounts her from her ottoman. The women laugh with her, and I do too, once I get it.

Spending many hours daydreaming about his homecoming, I think about what I will wear for him, something revealing but not a garish, skin-tight, brightly colored ultra mini tube dress suggestive of sausage casing. On more than one occasion while I wait at the pier, I watched women in this type of clothing struggle to keep themselves covered. Inevitably, a brisk wind off the Chesapeake Bay travels through Hampton Roads to the Norfolk Naval Base. Tube dresses do not do well in high winds. Either a woman is trying to keep it from blowing the dress off her breast or up her crotch, in which case, she is forced to cross her legs to keep the draft out. Add stiletto heels and big hair (it was the 80s) and you have the perfect storm. I must admit though, I admired the tenacity of the women who dared to pull it off.

I choose a long, loose fitting, heavy gauze dress that swishes from side to side as I stroll. It grounds me to the pavement, and I barely see my feet or the black leather flip flops I wear with it. It is bright royal blue at the top and bleeds out to the hem line to sky blue. It is sleeveless and low-cut. My height and toned upper body carry the dress, and my brown skin compliments the blue. I experiment with my hair: one night I curl, another I crimp, but in the end decide to wear it up given the heat and humidity of southern Virginia in July.

Thinking about the welcome home kiss stirs the energy racing through my body and ignites desire. I pretended to kiss him in our bed while I held his pillow against my chest, and I fell asleep many times with my lips pressed against it. I envisioned him taking my face into his hands and softly touching his lips to mine, a kiss of promise, the promise of what is coming once we are alone. We would hold hands as we leave the pier, our fingers interlocked tightly, purposely, as though we will lose each other forever in the crowd if we let go. I convinced myself that our reunion will more than compensate for our separation.

It is in the darkness I imagine I find the conjugal light I dream of for six months. Our bed is pristine: new, crisp sheets and clean linens pulled tightly, not a wrinkle in sight. I turn over the linens and ready the altar for lovemaking. I prepare for the ritual: bathing, primping and pruning until purified. I place my body ever so gently onto the bed and lie in wait. It is difficult to do, my practice is to reach for him with heightened energy, to wrap him in my arms and hold him tightly as though I am a python and he is my prey. I want him to make the first move, though; I want to be submissive, placid at first, but then aroused, inflamed, overwhelmed with passion, my senses heightened and then all inhibitions released. He comes to the bed, climbs in, and turns toward me. My back faces him. Desire is palpable, and I curl up and let it envelop me. As he runs his hand from my nape to the small of my back, my body unfolds and stretches like a cat laying on a Persian rug basking in the sunlight coming in through a window with a southern exposure. His palm migrates to my breasts, which he caresses before he follows the contour of my stomach, as though it is a roadmap to my womanhood. He rests here, and now he waits. On cue, I roll over, face him, and barely kiss his mouth. I run my fingers through his hair and down his neck, pausing at his nape to massage it, and then my palm comes to rest on his back. I reacquaint myself with his masculinity, stroking each muscle I encounter, squeezing, massaging, adoring. I bring him to me; his manhood seizes the moment, and I receive him with my eyes closed, with my third eye opened, and as we breathe in syncopated time, tease each other with gentle pecks and love bites and smile as we moisten each other's mouths with our tongues, I hope this proclivity will bear fruit. We are in our bed in a cocoon, and it keeps us safe from the outside world. Oh, how I toss and turn anticipating our reunion!

The post delivers a letter weekly, usually on Thursday or Friday. He is a better correspondent than I, but I write faithfully, sharing the neighborhood goings on, which are scant, or the latest news from our families, which is also scant. Even though his letters fill me with pride for his service to our nation, and I pay attention to the details of a mission I cannot fully comprehend, let alone relate to, what I want to read are words that echo my sentiments, my longings and desires for our life beyond military service, but to no avail. Service is his priority and will need to be mine as well, so I dedicate myself to a plan I create for us, intending to share it with him after he returns. I keep to myself and try to reign in superfluous feelings and thoughts, those that will not serve me as I serve a man committed to serving his country.

Our first anniversary pounces on me and thumps my sensibilities a few months after he deploys. June 2nd, 1986 should have been an evening for two to enjoy a quiet meal, an expensive bottle of champagne, sultry music, and each other's bodies. Instead, I sit at our kitchen table and dream about an experience I will never have with the man I love. I wait for loving words, an acknowledgement that one year has passed, but our first anniversary is a non-event. I am no longer a bride, and this makes me sad, but I do not know why. How could I know? I am a young woman filled with hope, so when the helicopter lands on the tarmac four months later instead of the pier, and he emerges in his flight suit, his helmet underneath his arm, striding to his XO, whom he salutes, and then to me, all is forgotten, the slate is wiped clean, and I anticipate what lies ahead. After all, I have a plan.

"We're leaving for South Dakota tonight." He opens the car door and tosses his kit bag onto the back seat. He pauses for a moment, "Are you getting in?"

"You just got home from sea. I don't understand." I open the car door as I look at him.

"I've got thirty days."

"Can we leave in a day or two? I want time alone with you."

"No."

"Why?"

"I want to go home. I've been at sea for months and I want to go home."

"We are home."

We get in the car, buckle up and ride in silence. He turns up the radio. I study his profile and survey his posture and the way he holds the steering wheel. He fiddles with his academy ring. Nothing. Expressionless, gaze straight ahead, a man with a plan different than mine. Outside my window, a parade of cars on 564 pass us, families and couples going home after months of separation, and I assume their reunions will be as I imagined mine would have been.

I scurry about at home collecting a few items to toss into a tote for a vacation I was not privy to, but he needs. He earned it, right? South Dakota is lovely, and we can make the trip our honeymoon. I can still have what I fixated on for months.

"How long is this drive?" I throw my tote in the jeep.

"About twenty-nine hours." He strips the jeep of its top, windows and doors.

"Where will we stop for the night?"

"Nowhere."

"Straight through, we don't stop?"

"We don't stop."

"Why?"

"We want to get there."

"Shouldn't we rest?"

"We'll rest when we get there."

"I don't think I can do it."

"We're not stopping."

"How about the top and doors?"

"It's summer, we don't need them… Did you grab my flight jacket?"

"No."

Our homecoming is over, traveling begins, but first we go to our credit union. While he is at the ATM, I stay busy rummaging through our totes and take inventory. I fear I don't have enough for thirty days, but I have my favorite dresses and casual sweats, so all is well. Besides, my in-laws have a washer and dryer. He packed just a few items: a couple of shorts and tees, bathing suit, and flight jacket. There is a heartfelt love coming through me as I scan our stuff, and I suggest to myself that I must be happy. We travel lightly; we don't need much to be comfortable. Our burden is relatively light. I have it all: husband, security, and youth. Children will follow, and this truth brings my notion of peace, and it is enough, and I think to myself, *I will make this trip memorable, like a proper honeymoon should be.* As I turn around and look forward, I see him as he takes the receipt from the ATM, crumples it up and throws it with force at the trash bin. He misses it, pauses, picks up the receipt and then slam dunks it into the bin while he shakes his head. The jeeps rocks as he gets in.

"There's no money in our account!"

"There's plenty. We get paid this weekend."

"What did you buy?"

"Nothing… I paid bills and bought food."

"We're broke."

"We get paid this weekend."

"So, we live paycheck to paycheck?"

"We'll be okay."

He fumbles with the key before shoving it into the ignition. It is locked, and he cusses it out before it relinquishes control and allows him to start the jeep. Grabbing its stick by its neck, he jerks it into reverse, backs up as if we are in mortal danger, slams on the brakes and shifts into first, then second and third. This compels him to brake hard at the parking lot exit, and we both feel our seat belts tighten. He makes a sharp right turn into the first lane when the traffic is clear. He hits the curb, and I grab the seat and hold on. I am in trouble. Big trouble.

The traffic on Interstate 64 heading west backs up as we approach the Hampton Roads Bridge Tunnel.

"Shit, I hope this doesn't take long."

He turns up the radio as we come to a complete stop. The late afternoon sun's heat weighs me down and siphons my reservoir of energy for itself.

"We didn't bring any water."

"Once we get to the mountains, it'll be nice. Hope you brought a jacket."

"I didn't know I needed one."

It takes an hour to make our way through the tunnel. By the time we stop for gas, I am parched, hungry and tired. While we wait for the tank to fill, he buys himself a Mountain Dew and chew. I get a Milky Way and a bottle of water after I use the women's room. We are on the road again in ten minutes.

"I want to be in Iowa by mid-morning," he says.

"It's starting to get cold." I put my sweatshirt on.

"It's going to get colder when we drive through the mountains."

"Are you sure we can't stop?"

"We can't afford a hotel room because we have no money."

"Let's use the MasterCard."

"No! You should have watched the money."

"I did. Our mortgage payment takes a lot of our pay. I paid bills and bought food."

"You bought plants."

"A few."

"What else did you buy?"

"Some clothes."

"My mess bill will be coming. We need to pay for that."

"Okay."

"We need to save money."

"We will."

"We can't afford to go to South Dakota." He pauses. "I should be able to go home after cruise."

"We are."

"We can't afford it."

Round and round we go.

"You need to not spend money." He bangs the palm of hand on the steering wheel.

"Please don't be angry with me."

"Then listen and don't spend money, nothing over fifty dollars unless we discuss it."

"Okay."

"You say 'okay', but you spend anyway."

"I bought plants."

"How much?"

"I don't remember, but it wasn't over fifty dollars."

"How do you know?"

"I know."

"But you don't remember."

Silence.

"See what I mean? No more! I want to be able to come home without worrying about money."

"I'm sorry. Can we get a room? I'm cold."

"You should have brought a jacket."

"I didn't know we were going through the mountains. Can I use yours?"

"I need it to drive."

"Please?"

"Next time you'll remember." He puts dip in his mouth and swallows a mouthful of Dew.

It is over. I huddle as best I can to keep warm, but without a top or doors, my efforts are futile. I look to him, then to the space between our seats. I unbuckle my seatbelt before I position myself on the floor between the two seats and on top of the transmission. The warmth from it permeates the floor and warms my bottom. I pull my sweatshirt over my knees and steady myself. The vibrating transmission soothes me, and I lean against the driver's seat. I fall asleep while he drives through the higher elevations of the Appalachians.

We arrive in Rapid City on schedule: twenty-nine hours from start to finish. Windblown and sun burned, I enter his parents' home. I wander to the bathroom to relieve myself but upon seeing my reflection in my mirror, I am horrified by my appearance. My long hair is matted, twisted and in knots; my eyes are bloodshot. I do my business and then without saying a word, sit at the kitchen table.

"No doors or top?" My father-in-law shakes his head.

"She's fine." He tosses his flight jacket on the sofa.

That evening I take a long, hot shower, scrub my body and wash my hair. After I detangle and dry it, I go to bed. I climb in it and consent as it swathes me in crisp, lined dried cotton sheets and an overstuffed comforter.

I curl up into a ball, close my eyes and breathe easily, thankful the drive is over. He comes in, undresses and sidles up to me. I stretch. No words are shared, our bodies speak for us. I am forgiven.

I ask in the morning, "Where are we going?"

"Hiking."

"Hiking? I don't have clothes."

"Mom has some you can borrow."

"Why didn't you tell me?"

"She has some."

"We'll need food," he says to Dad.

"Mom has all that."

"Okay, we'll leave in thirty minutes."

In the basement with Mom, I say, "This is a beautiful piece."

"It belonged to his grandmother… It was her china cabinet."

"It's lovely."

"One of these trips you can take it home with you." She gathers the clothing I need.

"Thank you, Mom." I run my hands along the edges of the cabinet imagining what I could do with it, perhaps convert it to a bookshelf or maybe a linen chest.

"Grab the cooler on your way up." Mom closes a box of clothes. "These will do for the hike."

"Thanks for letting me use them."

"It's no big deal."

I change. The shoes are one size too small.

"We're in God's country… what more could you want?" He drives up into the hills on Route 44.

"Those look like birch trees, and what kind of pine trees are those?" I point to the densely wooded area around me.

"Those are aspen and the pines are called Ponderosa."

"The aspen remind me of Massachusetts. We call them birch trees, though."

"You sound like a pilgrim." He laughs.

"Pilgrim? What do you mean?"

"That's what we call tourists."

"What's wrong with tourists?"

"They can't drive in the hills. They're a pain."

"They aren't that bad."

Silence.

I ask, "How long is the drive?"

"Not long."

"Are we driving there?"

"There aren't any roads to the summit. We'll hike from Sylvan Lake."

"How long is the hike?"

"About three miles"

"Is it hard?"

"Not really." He looks at me. "You can handle it."

"My shoes are too small."

"You'll be fine."

"What's up there?"

"A fire tower."

"We're hiking three miles to see a fire tower?"

"It's historic."

"How?"

"It's made of stone."

"And…"

"And the stone was hauled to the summit by mules and men."

"Okay, but I still don't get it."

"You'll see." He turns up the radio.

I am not prepared for the grandeur that is Harney Peak. As we draw closer to it, it fascinates me. Harney commands the hills, rising head and shoulders above anything else in its surroundings. His sentries, the incredibly tall and erect Ponderosas, muster and are at attention surrounding their sovereign. Though pliable, not even the breeze stirs them.

"It's awesome," I say.

"Of course, it is."

"Are we almost there?"

He does not answer; he rocks his body to Loverboy as they sing, "Everybody's working for the weekend… Everybody wants a little romance… Everybody's goin' off the deep end… Everybody needs a second chance…"

The hike to the peak is not arduous, but my feet are cramped, so it is difficult to keep up, but I take in the majesty of the hills and its prehistoric rock as I trudge on. The wildflowers: Rudbeckia, Echinacea, Penstemon, Queen Ann's lace and Bergamot pepper the landscape with a myriad of color, and they complement the rock formations, adding depth and richness to the overwhelming dark green that appears black. Birds sing and frolic among us living their lives in what must be heaven for them.

He walks several steps in front of me. He stands tall with his hands on his hips at the summit and gestures me to come to him using his head. He stands behind me.

"We can see four states from this point." He instructs, "To the west is Wyoming; to the south is Nebraska; to the northwest, Montana, and to the east South Dakota. God's country." He turns me around. "Over there is Mount Rushmore and just to the right are The Pinnacles."

"Pinnacles?"

"Needles Highway winds through them."

"You mean like the word?"

"Yeah, they're high pointy rocks."

"Are we going there?"

"We're going everywhere in the hills."

The nature reserve just beyond the learning garden is wet and filled with coastal flora; it has a strikingly different feel that The Black Hills. They are daunting, formidable, and varied; their contours work the senses, and its vastness takes a lifetime to grasp. The coastal plain possesses a serenity, perhaps because it is accessible, pleasant to the senses and easy to behold. I find myself on the bridge that crosses the creek into the reserve. Feigning interest in the marker that describes its habitat, I consider creation; its beauty does not go unnoticed, but it is not appreciated either; it is merely a backdrop I find apropos for the moment. A kingfisher in a loblolly pine perches. "Isn't that interesting," I say. "You're usually closer to water than this. You look a bit out of place, but you are a handsome one." And he is too, boyish in the early years, more distinguished now, a retired Captain with three responsible children and a wife who is happy to do for him. I think this is enough. Not him, though. He is unsettled, ill at ease and unreachable. Our communication stagnant, we recycle our words that have no meaning anymore, and they play in my head while I observe the Kingfisher fly from tree to tree.

"The bin is packed with beer cans again, and I found a kitchen trash bag full of empties under the counter in the garage."

"It's just a few beers."

"More than a few."

"Enough, Woman…"

"It's every night and all weekend."

"Stop bitching. You have it good."

"I know I have it good but…"

"Stop bitching."

I am stuck. I am, and as I consider my current situation, those fateful words come to the forefront. *One of those things… one of those things? Is this my marriage?* Butterflies flap in the pit of my stomach… the bad ones. I take my sunglasses off and try to discern a silver lining amid years of building clouds, but there is not one in sight; and as the sky darkens, I quicken my pace from the reserve and learning garden toward home while Shakespeare whispers in my ear, "Love bears it out, even to the edge of doom."

2

A Moment of Truth

Two days have passed since my son left. His father and I are alone in the house on either side of an invisible wall with one small door in the middle of it. I only open it if I need to. It is a bit overcast but still mild, and I stand at the window of a small room that is my safe place. Here I pace and talk to myself, trying to figure things out. The only problem is I cannot define "things." Last evening, while I lied in bed, a heavy thumping noise came down the hallway straight to me. It was a dark something: force, energy. It tried to attack me, but something shielded me. *Was that you, Daddy?* It is disturbing to contemplate the probability of darkness infiltrating my home. Did I imagine this? Where did it come from? Was it sent? Am I this vulnerable? What does this mean for us?

Reason tells me we can make it work now that the children are grown, no real worries anymore. Stable is the word most middle agers use to define their middle-class lives. This is us, stable. Reason says the issue has been pressure all these years while we raised them, and he built his career. It says he takes things out on me because he knows I am here for him—committed, and this is what a good and loving wife tolerates. Right?

His patience is gone, however, and I do not want to be scolded, so I comply with his wishes and avoid the family room which is his now.

Imagining life without him is difficult because it has been years since I have known a life of my own. I am inextricably tied to him. What recourse do I have, and even if I gather the strength to move on, how do I do it? He says, "You'll be bankrupt in two years without me." Maybe I will, so do I really want to go it alone? And how about love? It wants me to persevere and stay with him, but tired of making mistakes, saying the wrong things and walking on eggshells, I question it.

On my wedding day I had a clear understanding of what I thought was love. It was all about words: devotion, commitment, family. These I attached to the concept of it, and I was under the impression that living these words would naturally fill my life with it. It is as if *love* is out there waiting to be recognized and harnessed, and by some mystery of nature will *be* if tamed. Could it be a prescription to be followed with discipline, or boundaries; if maintained, love can survive, maybe thrive? Or is love something completely different, a force we cannot control and therefore should not try to, organic with its own pulse that needs to be understood from another perspective, one that I am not aware of?

What if I have spent a lifetime non-loving, and all my efforts with him have been measured poorly, so much so that we are at a point where we cannot square us away? My daughter and I replaced shelving in the pantry a few years ago, and in order for our work to pay off, we measured and measured again before we made any cuts or attached shelves to the walls. It was imperative we keep 90-degree angles throughout the project so the shelves were flush with each other. Did I not measure and remeasure my love for him? We are not flush, not even close, and as the marriage ages, the gap grows as it would with poorly placed shelving.

Do I know how to love him? I care and want him to be happy; I miss him when he is gone; and I desire closeness with him, but still, do these emotions mean I love him? The heroine of *Love* Story, Jenny, says, "Love means never having to say you're sorry," but I say it, and it has no impact. It is expected, and I am good at doing what is expected. Even so, I prefer love over reason because its hypnotic power is seductive, and I want to be seduced. It encourages me to release memories as a dam releases surplus water into a spillway. I acquiesce, as I always have, and it takes me away.

A stream of consciousness thought washes by with glimpses of life, and though brief, taken together each creates a colorful tapestry that is our family. I see blue and two shades of pink, each different-colored thread is a child whose birth enriches us. Our first fills life with curiosity and silliness. We were young and naïve, and he thought he knew how to bring our first into the world better than nature herself.

"This ought to help." He drives our CJ7 down a bumpy back road in Virginia Beach.

"I don't know."

"Sure, it will. You've been in labor all day. We'll move things along." He steers the jeep, hitting every rough spot along the way.

"Still ten minutes apart," I say after the ride is over.

"I hit some deep holes… huh, I thought that would do it for sure."

Our second weighs 7 pounds, 11 ounces, and is 21 inches long. He remarks, "I should have played the lottery: 7,11, and 21 are good numbers." Our third is overdue, and I am pushing forty and feeling the weight of this pregnancy.

"I forgot how much this hurts. It's been so long my body doesn't know what to do." I curl up in the front seat of our pickup as he drives to NAS Jacksonville.

"You're not far enough along to admit," the attending nurse says.

He shakes his head. "It took an hour to get here. We're not driving back."

"We'll wait here?"

"Not here. We'll go to the BOQ and get a room."

"They won't let me in, it's for officers only."

"They'll let us in." He grins.

"What?"

"This will be a story. At least there is room for you at the inn."

They grow and become little persons who endear themselves to me. "This?" The eldest asks as she positions Baby Dear. "On your nipple honey, not your belly button," I advise. "See how I have your baby sister." She gets off my lap, turns around and on tiptoes stares at her sister nursing. She leaves Baby Dear on my lap, puts her chair in front of me, takes off her top and places Baby Dear closer to her bosom.

"There," she says.

"You're a good mommy."

She wiggles. "How long?"

"Are you ready with the camera?" I ask before I light the candles on my second's cupcake. He nods and we sing.

"Blow out the candle!" her older sister commands.

She blows once, twice, three times.

"See? This is how you do it," big sister says as she blows them out. "Light it again, Mommy."

Little sister blows and blows and then sucks in her cheeks, collects as much saliva as she can and…

"No! Don't do that!"

"Can't do it, Sis."

"Just try."

She takes a deep breath, her cheeks inflate like a silicon balloon, and she blows.

"She can't do it!"

He picks up the cupcake and both girls blow it out. Delighted, they squeal, giggle, and play the rest of the afternoon. In the evening, after they are asleep, I bend over and put my arms around his neck. I kiss and bury my face there. He pats my arm, reaches for his beer, and drinks as he watches TV.

The youngest's obsession with dinosaurs becomes my obsession too. I learn habitats, species and pronounce seemingly incomprehensible words, and I hide creatures in his sandbox while he pretends he is a paleontologist.

"Mom, this is a stegosaurus. He's an armored dinosaur." He cleans the sand off his find before he places it on the porch floor. He then buries both hands in the box and explores until he happens upon his next discovery. "Plesiosaurus is a marine dinosaur. Do you know what that means?"

"Tell me."

"He lived in the ocean. Some people think he is the Loch Ness monster."

"Oh. Wow."

"Is there a raptor here?" Up to his elbows in sand and swishing his arms from left to right, he creates a dragnet by bringing them to his chest. "Got them!" He lifts Velociraptor, Dilophosauras and Archaeopteryx from the site. He scatters sand on the porch.

"Velociraptor is my favorite."

"I thought it was Allosaurus."

"I like him, but raptors are the best."

"Why?"

"They were smart. They talked to each other and hunted together."

"They were scary in Jurassic Park," I shudder.

He stands up, extends his arms, spreads his fingers and approaches. "Grrrr, grrrr, grrrr."

Crouching on my knees and covering my head with my arms, I am still with one eye open; then I spring up and scoop him in when he is in arms' reach. I lay him on my lap, cover his face with my open palm and move his head from side to side.

He howls, "Do it again! Do it again!"

We laugh together. "I could eat you up," I say.

"Like Velociraptor?" he says as I smother him with kisses.

"Why is that sand box still on the porch?" he asks as he walks in.

"He loves playing in it."

"It makes a mess." He opens a beer. "Isn't he too old for a sandbox?"

"He's four."

"It needs to go."

"Let it go, please."

"It makes a mess."

"I'll clean it up."

He relents, shrugging his shoulders as he walks upstairs, beer in tow, "Okay, whatever."

My second, who is five years old, and I ride bikes daily on a neighborhood path. It is lined with Live Oaks, and she is enamored with its moss.

"There's the special delivery." She sings as she reaches up to the tree and grabs a handful of it while she rides.

"Why is it 'special delivery'?"

"Because it's special, and I am delivering it to you."

"Want to race home?" I say.

"You can't catch me!"

The eldest and I spend time together throughout her junior year of high school while she competes in field hockey tournaments. We travel modestly: a clean room and small meals at the local Farm Fresh.

"Do you know what you want to do, honey?" I ask as I mix my salad.

"I like chemistry, but I don't know, maybe a doctor."

Before I eat, I look up at her with tears in my eyes. "You've done very well, top grades and test scores, you can be whatever you like."

She nods.

"I'm proud of you, and I love you."

Our eyes meet and we smile, "Thank you, Mommy. I love you too."

The youngest and I share a love for Star Wars. He reads journals, collects figures and paraphernalia, and reenacts favorite scenes in the family room. I surprise him one morning.

"Are you excited?" I ask after we get in the car.

"I can't wait!" he buckles up quickly. "It's going to be so much fun. Thanks for taking me out of school!"

"Should we get popcorn?"

He nods. "And a drink too?"

"Absolutely!"

"Here you go," a young man says as he gives my son a Mace Windu action figure while we wait to get inside the theater.

"Thank you!" He turns to me, his toothy grin beams. He holds up the figure. "This is the best day ever!"

Unforgettable sound bites vibrate through my mind. My eldest's famous words, "You're nothing but a whore on a power trip" chime in as well as my second's "You don't get it—you just don't get it," yelled at me in frustration through tears and a dramatic exit from the kitchen to her bedroom; and the youngest's mantra throughout high school, "I got it Dude," competes for attention.

They challenge my authority, sometimes taking me to the edge of sanity. In those moments I am on my own, and my response determines my sovereignty during his absence.

"Don't you do it."

"I don't care what you say. I'm old enough to go!"

"Don't you do it." I run down the stairs.

"I'm leaving!"

"No, you're not!"

The others hear the commotion, come out of their rooms and watch. I put myself between the doorknob and her.

"You're going nowhere!".

She looks at me while reaching her hand out. "No! Don't even think about it!" She backs down, and I close the deal. "Get upstairs now!" She stomps off.

We have pizza picnics in the family room, summer days at the base pool, dance parties in the kitchen and lots of treats. We shop at the commissary together, and I pretend I do not know they snuck items into the grocery cart. We are our best as a family during the holidays.

He prefers tall, fat trees, Douglas firs. He takes time to trim it and set it in the tree stand straight and secure. "Even the cat can't knock it down," he says. The children and I decorate it early on, but as they grow, it is my thing, and I love it because the tree hosts their creations, mementos of childhood made with love and lots of glitter and glue. He chooses our meals and puts together a detailed schedule I follow. "The meat is not going to be ready on time... my projection on the computer doesn't match the meat thermometer... I screwed up." His annual pronouncement is not taken seriously because the meat is always delicious. I prepare all side dishes, my mashed potatoes a perennial favorite. He and I prepare soups, too. By the time the children are young adults, they cook with us. The eldest orchestrates our holiday with a master schedule written out on a whiteboard which is color coded: one for time, another for the dish, still another for our names. Our culinary responsibilities are based on our expertise in the kitchen.

We take our seats, he and I at the heads of the table and I lead the blessing. "In the name of the Father, the Son, and the Holy Spirit. Bless us Lord and these thy gifts, which we are about to receive, from thy bounty, through Christ our Lord, amen… In the name of the father, son, and the Holy Spirit." Wine is poured, and we feast, share, and laugh. We do a lot of this on the water as well.

We explore it with our children: the Poquoson River, Back River, and York River. We creep through creeks and venture out to the Chesapeake Bay, as far as the Bay River Bridge Tunnel, to fish a couple of times. We sashay along the Severn and the intercostal waterway takes us to St Augustine many times.

"Do you see that?" I point out to the middle of the waterway.

"Where?" Without sunglasses, he struggles.

"Port side, what is that?" I point again.

"It's a manatee. Look, girls." He slows the boat to "no wake" speed.

"What's wrong with its top?" the eldest asks.

"Propeller got it," he says. "They get maimed and killed every year colliding into boats."

"Poor creature." I squat and peer over the side to get a better look. "Hard to believe sailors thought they were mermaids."

The girls turn their heads to each other. "It doesn't look anything like Ariel," the younger one says.

We spend hours tubing. Their bodies bounce along; their hair is wet and wild; their grins are wide. Living life on the water is our pastime; we raise our children there until their lives become their own, and then, being together is an event, not a way of life, like he and I. My mind pauses for a moment, and I lean my forehead against the window. Outside the birds gather around the only filled feeder. I breathe in… I breathe out, and then I wipe my breath's impression off the window. "Love" cautions me not to close the spillway yet. I want to, but without the strength required, I let go of the hydraulics and my thoughts continue to flow.

He is a junior officer when we join the HSL (Helicopter Squadron Light) community. I help him study NATOPS often, quizzing him on emergency procedures mostly, but also on information he needs to deposit into long term memory. Many evenings after supper, I sit with him and review.

"General Characteristics," I say, but then pause and read silently.

"I'm waiting."

"Sorry. Length?"

"52 feet 7 inches."

"Rotor diameter?"

"44 feet."

"Height?"

"15 feet 6 inches."

"Disc area?" I yawn.

"1520.53 square feet," he says, "Can you go faster?"

I pick up the pace. "Empty weight, max take-off weight?"

"7,040 pounds, 12,800 pounds." He takes a swig of beer. "Faster."

"Max speed, cruise speed, range, service calling, rate of climb?"

"143 knots, 130 knots, 366 miles, 22,500 feet, 2,070 feet/minutes with two auxiliary fuel tanks at sea level, 1,305 feet/minutes with one engine sea level," he rattles. "Faster."

I sit up straight, turn, and face him at the other end of our couch. "Hover in ground, out, max range, max endurance?"

The numbers roll off his tongue without effort. "17,600 feet, 14,600 feet, 450 nautical miles with two auxiliary fuel tanks, 4.5 hours at 5000 feet." He finishes his beer.

"Cost?"

"12 million, but I don't need to know this."

"Show off!" I wrap my arms around him as he passes by.

"We'll go over emergencies next, after I get a beer."

"You know the protocols."

"Get ready." He smiles.

I hear the words "I love you" at his changes of command and retirement ceremony, but he does not look at me when he utters them. What I think is the "I love you" of our marriage is carried by the flow of memories. It floats on top of them and sits there, bobbing. This memory has sustained me through the years, though as of late, it is fleeting and weak.

"Are you okay?" His voice trembles.

"I'm scared. What if they come back?"

"Don't worry about that. They were runaways... they took what they wanted."

"I have the .22 next to me." I lean down from the side of the bed and stroke the walnut stock of his hunting rifle.

"Is it loaded?"

"No."

"It's not going to do you any good not loaded."

"I have a good swing; I'll use it like a bat."

Silence

"Are you there?"

"I'm coming home right now. I'll be there in fifteen hours. I love you." Fifteen hours he drove, through the night and into the morning hours to get home and protect his family; and that evening, after I put the girls to bed, I had the homecoming I dreamt of when I was a bride.

The tapestry of memories has oranges, yellows, greens, brown and some gold, too. These colors are reminders of our professional successes as well our children's milestones. Our life is comfortable; though not without challenges, it is relatively pedestrian, and our children are safe. Can something so beautiful be dismissed like the project of a grade school kid not artistically inclined? Can we relegate our art to the ash heap, discarded and out of site? Beyond the vibrancy of color, at the foundation of the work, the horizontal threads blend with the vertical threads on the loom of life; and it is there I see it... the lack of tamping, that crucial step needed to weave the threads together tightly to create a lasting work of art. My body recoils, and I garner the fortitude to close the spillway. I am not at ease.

A swell of emotion rises like a storm surge and tears flood my face. He left our bed more than a year ago. "I can't sleep with the radio on," he tells me, but when I turn it off, he does not come back. "It's better in the other room," he decides. For years he has been emotionally distant, now physically unavailable. Even when I try to be tender, I remember his touch and his arms around me, and I crave both. He calls me Slim anytime I reach for a snack and says, "It doesn't matter how much exercise you do; you'll always have a fat ass." God, I feel ugly.

Overcome with a heavy heart, I do not want to break up the family, though. Why should they endure it? Grandchildren will be coming in the next few years and staying together for them is a good thing as well. But looking around for the first time, I realize my personal life is relegated to a small room upstairs that was once a nursery. In it I have a small table, desktop computer, favorite books and keepsakes: my daughter's dented rain stick, her sister's lopsided pottery and their brother's incomplete sketches of galactic warriors. This is my world currently, and it is time to think it through because I am a fifty-three-year-old woman who squats in her own home.

The teachings of the Church invade my mind, jumbling everything together which is unsettling because for years they have been a source of comfort. They remind me it is sinful to contemplate ending my marriage: divorce puts a practicing Catholic in direct opposition to the foundation of the faith. "What God has joined let no man put asunder." These words keep looping in my head, a never-ending reminder of commitment. I cover my ears and scream inside, *What about Ephesians, the part where Jesus says a man should love a wife as he loves his church? That counts too! I did my part! I submitted to him!* I wait for an answer and it comes. We promised; we swore on a bible; we entered a covenant with God. Pray… I need to pray and offer us up to the Blessed Mother.

Standing at the window watching the birds on the feeder out back, my resolve slowly dissipates like a New Year's resolution. Can we make it, really? We struggle and at the heart of it is me, at least that is what he thinks. I "need instruction," and do not "think logically." I cannot be trusted with important decisions. "Don't worry your pretty little head about it," he says. "It's better for me to take care of it." My attitude toward money is lax as far as he is concerned; and when I say, "God will take care of us," he is angry and says, "Will he pay the bills?!" I fret and I am told we will never retire and have a good life when we are old, but I look around and see our peers and they are fine. I do not trust myself to make important money decisions, and I know he does not want me to spend it, and I do not unless he is away. I don't make any life decisions. I take care of the children's everyday lives only.

Sharing my space is an old cabinet given to us by his mother. Over the years it has had many purposes including a gun cabinet he fashioned out of it, but no more. It sits empty, lonely, forlorn. As I stare at, its cry for purpose is heard and without much deliberation I decide I need a distraction, a creative outlet. "You'll make a fine bookcase," I say.

He is sitting on the couch scrolling through Facebook while he watches TV and drinks. I pause at the threshold to the family room before I tiptoe past him and through the garage door. It takes time to close it behind me without making any sound. I do not want him to know what I am up to; and as I collect the hammer and screwdriver it pains me to think there is so much distance between us and I sneak around, like a child whose afraid her actions will get her in trouble, after so many years of marriage, but I cling to hope and those emotions that manipulate me, for I am the marionette dependent on the will of my puppeteer; and I pause before I open the garage door because I am aware that I just had an insight, a clue about me, and I make a mental note, though it gets lost amid the disarray of information that is my thought process.

Back upstairs, I clear a space on the floor for the cabinet by moving books, the table and chairs. My movements are imperceptible to him, and I make sure to shut the nursery and master bedroom doors so he does not hear me when I begin working on the task at hand: removing the ammunitions box he screwed onto the top of the piece. Before he claimed it, I stripped and re-sanded the oak. Its simple design and unassuming manner is its allure, and it resided in my kitchen for several years while he lived in Florida. He altered the original piece when he attached the box to the top of it with mill lumber. There is a problem: the screws are secure and counter sunk. I pry with all my might and end up taking the box as well as the top of the cabinet off. I fall back on the floor with a thud and the wood does too. Footsteps pound up the wooden staircase; they are in rapid succession and loud.

"What the hell are you doing!"

"I'm making the gun cabinet into a bookcase." I hunch over.

"Who said you could do that?" He staggers toward me.

"You're not using it…"

"You think you can do anything you want! You're a real cunt that way!" He stands over me; rage distorts his face. I cover my head with my arms and keep silent. Out of the corner of my eye I see him make a motion to strike me, but he does not and storms out of the room instead. I pick up the cabinet and take it to his bedroom with the intention of never going near it again. He watches from the bottom of the stairs and it is clear he is troubled by his behavior.

The look on his face gives me the courage to confront him. It is in his eyes, and I see it as he stands there and looks up at me. It is not anger, but I am not sure what it is either. I come from his bedroom hoping he is still there, but he is back on the couch. I hear the crack of a beer can opening. From the balcony, I reach out to him.

"Are you ready to stop drinking and go into counseling?"

Silence.

"Please! Please answer me… are you ready?"

Silence.

"You need help! I need help! Let's get help! We're losing each other!"

Silence.

"You're becoming an alcoholic!"

Silence.

"Are you listening?"

"I know I am! I don't care!"

His words are my bellwether. Time stops; it contracts and closes in, and the floor beneath me is a whirlpool. I swim; my arms are frantic, and I gasp for breath, and I cannot swim against it. As I slip away, deeper and deeper until all around me is water, I lose sight of him. What am I supposed to do? I grab hold of the railing as I begin to shake. "Why did you marry me?"

"I have no idea!"

Silence. "Now what?"

"We can be civil to each other."

"Do you love me?"

"You don't want to give up Starbucks… and don't forget the grandkids… you don't want them to have to choose."

"Do you love me?"

"Don't you want to be comfortable?"

"I want to be loved."

"You'd rather have love than comfort?"

"Do you love me?"

"I could if you listened and do as I say, but you don't."

"After all these years…"

Silence.

"I appreciate you were honest with me before we got married, but I should have known I couldn't spend my life with someone whose character is flawed like yours," he says.

"Why am I still being punished for that? I was 19!"

Silence

"Your cousin had one. Why is it okay for her?"

Silence

"I can't do this anymore," I say.

"You'd rather have love than comfort?"

"I'd rather have love and work harder."

"Whatever."

"I gave you my youth! I had potential!"

"Without me you'd be working at a radio station making twenty grand a year."

I walk to him, swing my arm as forcibly as I can and send the end table lamp across the room. Our eyes meet, and for a moment the world around us fades away, and I think, *so this is how our marriage dies.*

3
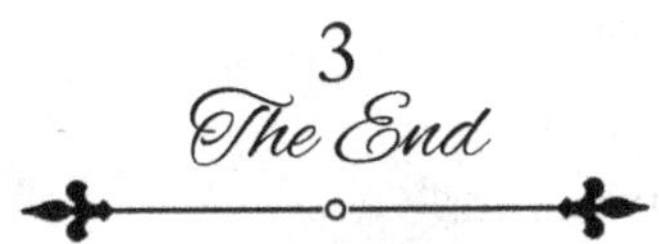
The End

Our thirtieth anniversary is here, and my husband wishes me a "Happy Anniversary." Unsettling because I have not heard these words from him for many, many years; the text hangs there, tiny strands of twine suspend from it to nowhere, yet he manipulates it, taunts me and bears down when I am most at risk. It has been a few days since I launched the lamp across the room. We still live under the same roof.

There is a presence in the house, a tumor that languishes. It appears benign, and I do not pay much attention to it since he and I are, ostensibly, working through the legalities of divorce. But something changes, and I realize I misdiagnosed the growth; it is malignant, and it lashes out at me through him.

"What the hell is taking your lawyer so long?"

"I don't know."

"She's useless! Why didn't you listen to me? Oh, wait a minute, you never do, that's right. How long is this damn divorce going to take?"

"What does it matter?"

"I have a golf tournament in July."

"What?"

He laughs.

"Do you have plans?"

"What's it to you?"

"Just curious…"

"Don't be! You want out—you're out!"

"You want it too. What about your dad?"

"What about him?"

"I want to come there when the time comes. Is this okay with you?"

"I'll ignore you if you come."

"Is this how it's going to be?"

"Are you changing your name?"

"Yes."

"Have you told the kids?"

"No."

"Can't wait to hear what they think."

"I think they'll be okay."

"Might as well. You don't deserve my name."

"No, I don't."

"What does that mean! It served you well."

"I don't dislike the name, I just want mine back. I didn't want to change it in the first place."

"Just as well in case I marry again."

"You want that?"

"Yeah, I might want to."

"I can't even think about it."

"You're going to be just like your mother."

He chooses to stay, and I do not ask him to leave. We coexist with the growth that I recognize has been with us for years but was latent, and I did not see its symptoms anyway because I put my faith in "love." Now it is out of control and no treatment can prolong its inevitability; it will metastasize. Nothing will be left but the shell of a marriage, and my hopes for some semblance of a relationship for the good of the family dims.

"I can't wait to get out of here and back to South Dakota! This place sucks!"

"But your son is still here in school."

"I'll deal with my son. Stay out of it!"

"We're his parents. We need to work together."

"I'll deal with him without you!"

"I want to try and have something to hold the family together."

"If he needs something, he can get in touch with me."

"Please…"

"I'll let the kids judge for themselves."

As the days unfold, we take what is ours. He collects what he wants from the kitchen, family and back rooms, and I watch him as he shoves all his books into a garbage bag. He comes to me. "The Harley stool is mine."

"I know. I gave it to you for Christmas."

"Are you keeping it?"

"No, it's yours." I get off it and carry it to the garage. "I won't sit on it again."

"And I need thirty-two thousand dollars from our account?"

"Why?"

"I'm buying a trailer."

"Oh?"

"And since this is going to be my home and you get the house, I think this is fair."

"Okay."

"And I'm buying a new truck to haul it."

"Whatever you need."

"And I decided I want some of the investment money."

"But we agreed…"

"I can't get that back."

"I'll need retirement money then."

"Why?"

"Because it's fair."

Later that day we are outside. I am in the garden, he is in the garage sorting through his tools, fishing gear and collection of salvaged material. As I cross the driveway, I look to him and he says, "What?"

"Nothing."

He turns and walks up the stairs that lead to the family room, but before he goes inside he turns back. "I am your pinnacle. You'll never do better than me."

Retirement pay is the issue with us, and I go back and forth with my attorney, who cautions me to think with my head. I cannot, his words reverberate within. "I can see if you went to the academy and then stayed home with the kids, but you didn't. You did nothing to earn any of it." I feel like an ancient amphora baking in the hot Roman sun wanting ambrosia.

Can't this all go away? Can't we start again?

"Do you hear me?" my lawyer asks.

"I'll have to sell the house," I say.

"Yes."

"I don't know. My son is still young."

"He wants you to have…"

"Nothing, but ten percent he thinks is fair."

"And you?"

"I don't know. Maybe twenty with everything else."

"Take at least twenty-five."

"He can have all the retirement if he gives me everything else, but he changed his mind. We had this settled."

"He talked to someone."

I lock myself in one of the spare bedrooms at night as the growth meanders about. I read for a bit, but mostly listen for him, or any sound or misplaced step that keeps me on edge. Reruns of episodes of our marriage are broadcasted in my mind, and I do not pay attention to them anymore; their lessons are lost or incomprehensible, and it is as though I am trapped on a sofa whose springs are shot. It takes effort to get up and walk away; and even if I could, I cannot get up. I am bound to it with profound sadness, and I soak in it until my skin shrivels.

I hear a thud. He is there, midway up the stairs against the wall. He trips again on his way to the top. An eerie feeling comes over me and I am compelled to ask, "Where are the handguns?"

"They're fine."

"Where are they?"

"Not here."

"Your rifles are still in the closet?"

"What about it... Oh! I get it." He passes out of step, eyes fixed to mine and then into the spare bedroom. I follow. "I don't have any bullets, but it's okay," he says as he holds the gun up. "Besides, it's not together."

The look on my face probably conveys my fear and lack of trust. He laughs. "You're not worth it!" The following evening, I pack an overnight bag and go to a hotel. I sneak out of the house like a rebellious teenager on a school night. How does he know that I am gone? He never checks on me, but this night he does, and he messages me asking what is going on. I message back that I need space. The following day, he asks my opinion about a letter of resignation he has drafted. He reads it to me.

"I'd keep it upbeat."

"Who cares?"

"You don't know how you'll feel in a year or so. They are your recommendation."

"That's enough. Be on your way." He raises his hand and shoos me away as though I am a pesky fly.

A general air of malaise lives with us too, but it does not impact him. I am particularly susceptible to it, however; apparently, my emotional immune system is weak, and though one might assume it breeches my being because of the separation, I am not sure. Weakness runs deep; it skulks in the shadows triggered by events. The separation agitates it and brings it to the forefront, but it has been with me for a lifetime, and I have no idea how to cope with it.

I drift through the house aimlessly running my hand along the dusty chair railing. I follow it around the room until I reach the French doors separating it from the parlor, and then I follow it around the parlor. It leads me to the back room, which is no longer used now that the children are grown. In there are memories of halcyon days, calmer seasons. They lay under white coverlets now to protect them while I sort out this current one. My legs take me to the window that overlooks the bog garden as they have many times over the years.

The tall, flat leaves of flag irises gather in a small, moist space creating a habitat for the rat snake, and I try to discern if there is one amongst them, but since the leaves do not rustle, there probably is not. The beautiful and dainty yellow flower is its appeal, and it has not bloomed in years because I have not divided it. Had I known its rhizomes cannot be divided without a sharp axe and brute strength, I may never have planted it; nevertheless, I have grown fond of its foliage's intrinsic beauty. To its left are a few marsh hibiscuses. Their pink flowers are not nearly as attracted as their seed pods, which I use for my holiday arrangements. In the distance stands swamp sunflower, and she is nearly as tall as I, yes, close to five feet five inches; and her yellow blossoms brighten a corner of the garden as if a hundred miniature suns rest on her stems. And there, coming out of the shallow pond through the green, is purplish blue pickerelweed. I prefer liastris or gayfeather whose flowers are similar in structure and color, but they do not survive in my garden despite my best efforts. The cattails are struggling, and I chastise myself for trying to transplant them when I know once they are settled in, they do wish to be disturbed.

Between the bog garden and the woodland is a patch of wet earth covered with pine straw. I visualize a large pond there surrounded with water loving native plants like the ones I have now: hibiscus, swamp sunflower, iris etc., and I want to add Indian grass, blue vervain, lilies and lotus flowers. Around the perimeter are rock formations, at one end built up to allow a small waterfall to cascade into the pond to keep the water churning and the mosquitoes to a minimum. Among them I plant several varieties of sedum and after several years they fill the nooks and crannies and cover the rocks and create soft squishy mounds of texture and color. Mosses, too, a variety of them, for they do well in my wet, shady garden. There is koi… well, probably goldfish to begin because there is the threat of predators above that will swoop down and take what is mine for themselves. In time, the water garden takes on a life of its own, like the butterfly garden has, and I receive its gifts: life, harmony, and beauty, and all it asks of me is to pull the weeds around it and prune the plants it supports once a year. These thoughts are soothing, yet immaterial. The water garden lives within, not without, and although there is no telling that it will ever actually exist in my garden, it is mine nonetheless, very much like an oil painting that inspires. I like to think Monet would appreciate it too.

Out of the corner of my eye I see red, in the bog garden that is, which is unusual because I have not planted a red blooming plant there. I strain my eyes until I see it clearly. Cardinal flower! What a joy! I smile and hurry to the dining room window. From there I see its mother, my crowning achievement in the front garden, a multi-stemmed red cardinal flower a couple of feet tall blooming. She is surrounded by *Vinca* and *Rudbeckia* that relocated from the butterfly garden a couple of years ago. If I am patient, hummingbirds will soon come; and so, for a moment I wait and set aside separation, divorce, paperwork and all the emotional baggage that comes with those things. I shelter the moment, as though it is a cold New England winter's night, and promise myself that one day I will feel as I do right now, and it will not be a momentary occurrence; it will be a mindset.

I watch from the stoop as he packs for his journey back to the Black Hills. There is a homecoming waiting there for him, an inevitable destination to reunite body with being, and I see it, really observe what has been apparent from the beginning, and I am not a part of it... never have been.

"I could love you," he says, "but you don't listen." I'm holding the loppers, poised to prune, and honestly, I do not want to prune unless it is necessary. Plants should not be constrained; they should have the room to grow as they need to, unencumbered by my limitations to envision them as they are and meant to be in their natural habitat. I manage to clip an aberrant limb off the Nandina before he slams the tailgate of his F150 closed. *Could love me? When did you stop?*

"Are we going to compete or cooperate for holidays?" He raises his hands, posturing as though his question is of consequence.

I open and close the loppers. *Listen? To what? To whom?* "It's for the best," I say.

"It is because you won't..."

Because you won't. How long have I heard this refrain? For years. "It's your fault, too." I suppose there are words I need to say, but I am all out of them. Thirty years' worth of them is not enough for him to want to make us work, and I am just too tired to care anymore. He starts the truck, shifts into reverse and backs away slowly. I hear the gears shift again, he drives away, and that is that.

When he is out of sight I collapse on the stoop. I sigh and startle a tree frog lounging on a daylily leaf. He hops into the dwarf pussy-willow, and I lose sight of him in its gnarled branches and chartreuse foliage. Focusing on the joint between the front porch and the brick stairs, I notice the concrete in the joint is crumbled. Picking up bits of it without thought, I leave a cavity I have no intention to fill. I cup them in my left hand and stir. My thoughts reach back and remind me about the times I pretended my left hand was a pot and bits of rock were the ingredients to a stew I made for a make-believe husband when I was a girl. The glaring difference is my fantasy husband loved me and did not leave. I cease mixing and pick up one bit at a time and rub it between my thumb and index finger before it plops back into my left palm. *Why didn't you love me? Why didn't you tell me? And how do I manage this alone?* I close my left hand and shake the bits before I toss them in the flower bed. They scatter in the vinca minor.

I watch the sun climb into the Virginia sky from the parking lot at Messick Point the morning after he leaves. The drive to the point is uninteresting until I pass the residences at the end of Messick Road. Before the bend I have a view of Back River to my right and Front Cove to my left. Beyond Back River is Langley Air Force Base and NASA, one a reminder of American power, the other a source of American pride and innovation. The hushed sounds of the cove call me, and the pungent odor from the salt marsh infiltrates through the window and I follow it to the sea wall.

The sun pauses on its mount and rests among a gathering of cirrus clouds. They envelop it as a mother does her precious child when he awakens from a peaceful nap. *I have my children, and they are the beauty in my life.* A great blue heron traverses the horizon, floating effortlessly with the air current side to side lulling itself as it eases into another day. *Now what?* The sun breaks free of the clouds, and by the time it reaches its summit, Messick is awake.

Below, the water sloshes; falling into its rhythm, I slosh too. I am water: colorless, odorless, tasteless. Two seagulls squawk incessantly, posturing on adjacent pilings. As they take flight toward Poquoson River, a small flock of egrets approach. They cruise toward the salt marsh, wings extended, plumage fringed. Their black legs out in front and their web feet flexed, they glide along the surface of the water for an instant before sinking gracefully until their bodies take rest on the water's surface. They perch... we perch and wait. For me it is a hint, a clue with direction I seek, a way to begin mid-life without a script. Are they a clue? Their serenity and confidence I lack. The seagulls know the way out from their shelter to the great Chesapeake Bay and back again. Maybe their way of life is a hint I need to consider moving past all this. I am not convinced I can find my way either forward or backward. I have no bearings, not sure which direction is true north. The sun rises; the clouds dissipate; the birds emerge from their nests. Where do I fit? My life is blurry currently, and what is in focus is indistinct.

Does life move forward without recourse, repentance, or regret? I am life. What is my recourse? My life path is a dead end now. Drunk on love's elixir, I could not see, and I did not listen to my heightened senses. I chose to enter the labyrinth of romance and passion, and I am stranded there. How do I break free of it? If I had the proper tools, this is one time I would prune, not hack my way out, but I suspect this solution is not the best choice. And how do I repent for breaking an unbreakable sacrament? I do not dare think about this right now because it is too much to reconcile my choice with eternal life. Will someone throw me a life ring? Except for my children, I am drowning in a sea of regret.

The mullet forage close to the surface of the water and in the near distance the bait fish rustle, creating a near perfect circle of rippling water amid what otherwise appears to be glass. Watermen begin to draw near; their deadrises, though worn and aged from years of navigating through the precarious waters of the Chesapeake Bay, cut through the water with ease. Some are packed with crab pots, others are empty, their lode somewhere out in the bay harvesting blue crabs for us. I turn my back to them and my eyes drift until they find insects mingling with the dill along the water's edge. Soon the Swallowtail will lay her eggs on its leaves and the transformation will begin. Perhaps another clue? Hint? Even if it is, it is of no use. I am broken.

What happened… what happened! How did we get to this? I loved you. I still love you… but you don't love me. I bore three children… bodies change, yours did too, but I still wanted you, why not me! You left our bed, pushing my love away like it was a contagion, even when we went away together. Anger… your anger… what did I do? I don't understand! The spinning continues. *What is wrong with me… not together… not enough for you… and where am I… alone in a southern town still learning to dance like southerners… away from my people… family… children. You said my character is flawed… mistaken to think you could spend your life with me.* My heart plummets. *Why torment me? No way out. I confided in you… you knew everything about me, but I wasn't safe with you! I can't forget the comments… the names. I can't look in the mirror! I am your pinnacle; you can't do better. Why say this?* I choke up. *Make this all go away! Please! Please take this pain from me!*

I hunch over, tuck my chin to my knees. My hands cover my ears to stifle the din in my head. My palms are a vice tightening their hold on my head, trying to drown it all out while I try to salvage my dignity and apprehend his words that assault my heart. I release my head, my ears pop and my hands tingle. *Thirty years, and it's over! Why can't I cry?*

The rumbling of a F350 diesel with a fishing boat in tow approaches taunting the mounting turmoil within, announcing that Messick is now a recreation hub, and I prefer it in the quiet of dawn. As I drive away, I spy the egrets whose coordinated flight into the cloudy blue sky over Messick Point inspires nothing, but I wait for them to fly out toward Poquoson River anyway before I return to an empty house and a shattered life.

<h1 style="text-align:center">4
Bottoming Out</h1>

There are numerous squatters in my brain posing as unanswered questions. I envision them in close quarters, bunked, some three or four high assembled on the left side of my brain jockeying for position and power. The right side reacts to their presence: It suffers from a dire lack of creativity, intuition, and balance. The two sides battle each other, leaving me physically drained and emotionally stifled. I subject myself to his lover's constant posts of them, fully embedding the knife in my back, twisting it, making certain I feel pain again and again, convinced somehow I was the one who brought on the divorce.

I wander. First around the garden lamenting my disregard for its appearance, knowing the feeders are empty and winter will be here soon, leaving the blue birds no hope to find sustenance in my yard when the snow moves in. Then I begin to venture out to nowhere special, a park or a museum… wandering, not experiencing until I wander the coastline at Buckroe Beach. There, I take in the refreshing air coming in from the bay. Facing the vast mass of water, I lock into the healing energy radiating from it, feeling it permeate my body, and I am reminded of biology class and the notion of osmosis, and I know this is what's happening. A sense of equilibrium allows the cleansing breath, and I sit down. There are the familiar sounds: the ebb and flow of water, the chirp of the birds, the whisper of wind through the air; but then, in an instant, the distinct sound of rotating helicopter blades severs my connection to it, and I curse it and him as I dig my feet into the sand and twist them on my way back to the car. A few days later, I find myself in a Harley showroom, as if I have been whisked away by an invisible force and placed in this spot without my consent, but it is okay because it is meant to be.

The salesman finds me staring at a turquoise heritage softail. "She's a beautiful machine," he says.

"She is."

"Interested?"

"I don't know why I'm here."

Silence.

"My husband and I rode before we split."

"It's rough."

"Do I miss riding, or do I miss him?"

"Maybe both," he says as I leave.

That evening I stand in front of the mirror, and I do not look at its reflection, but I ramble the same musings I've had since this started. *What is wrong with me? I was nothing to you, just a woman… What did I do to make you hate me so much? I tried to be good and listen and not spend a lot of money. I can't believe you want her over me.*

I walk into the bedroom and free fall onto the bed, face down.

What does she have that I don't? She's a fucking drinker! You like that though, and stupid me tried to be one too, and when I quit, you said, "You were just starting to be fun." She's more fun than I could ever be I guess, and she's skinny, and we know you really like that and that fake blonde hair. You're there having fun all the time, and I'm here in this house that is a mess and needs so much work before I can sell it. I made it too easy, and I let you treat me so poorly. All of it for love… fucking love! You ruined everything! We were supposed to be better… we were supposed to make it! I can't go to church anymore. Well, fuck, I don't want to, but I love Christ and the Blessed Mother; I want them in my life.

My words are unproductive, all my questions unanswered, and I cannot help but think something is quite wrong with me, maybe fundamentally, a hidden mental illness I am not aware of but now is manifesting. I put the kettle on and after the chamomile is steeped, I sit on the porch sofa, close my eyes and envision what I want life to be, but I do not have the grounding to manipulate the noise within. My body is throwing a rager, and though invited, I do not want any part of it. I can only hope the tea will sedate and relieve me of it.

I speak to my sister on the phone daily and I have a one-track mind. I marinate in thoughts of him and our marriage. I am a played-out record still on the turntable, spinning while the needle scratches the vinyl redundantly. Our conversation is predictable, rote, much like grammar lessons.

"Are you okay, Sis?" she says.

"I don't know." I flop down on the sofa.

"What are you doing?"

"Staring out the window at the empty feeders."

"Have you eaten?"

"Enough."

"What's enough?"

"Oatmeal."

"Lunch?"

"I'm not hungry."

"Sis! What are you thinking?"

"I'm fucked up."

"This isn't about you."

"Isn't it?"

"It's about him."

"He's moved on."

"Stop!"

"What happened?" I sit up.

"He wanted out."

"Why?"

"Does it matter?"

"I need to know."

"There were issues."

"I know, but…"

"Don't you think this is best?"

"I thought we'd be okay in the end, even though there were issues."

 "Why?"

"I thought he loved me. I love him, and I thought the years apart and his drinking were the reasons, not our feelings toward each other."

"Please, stop."

"Why did he stop loving me? What did I do? He told me he had no idea why he married me."

"Sis…"

"How did I live with a man for thirty years and not have a clue?"

"Sis…"

"Where the hell have I been?"

"You've been focused on your children."

"Still…"

"There's no sense rehashing thirty years. It's over now."

"And now, her!"

"Stop. Come to grips."

"With what?"

"Your reality."

"Reality is an illusion."

"Don't go there with me."

"My reality was my marriage."

"Your reality was warped."

"What?"

"You think I'm blind? You think I didn't know?"

"Know? What? What did you know, oh wise one?"

"You got crumbs from him, that's all. He wasn't there for you. Now and again he'd give you his attention and you ate it up, but then he'd dismiss you."

"I don't see it."

"You didn't see it because you knew nothing else. You weren't appreciated.

You were expected to do and that's it, no more. Once in a long while he'd acknowledge you and that was enough for you. You didn't demand anymore."

"I'm not sure I want you to say anything more about my marriage."

"Are you defending him?"

"No, maybe, I don't know."

"Well, I do."

"So, now you're an expert on marriage?"

"I'm on your side."

"I tried, Sis. I'm sorry."

"No more apologies, no more! You've spent years saying sorry for no reason!"

"Okay, *okay*."

"You need to let him go."

"How? I love him."

"You need time."

"I'm confused."

"You need time."

"I look at Facebook and I see the man I married, and he looks happy with his life, as if he's lived in South Dakota for years."

"Get off that site!"

"Do you think he's happy?"

"I don't care about him or his happiness, and I wish you didn't either."

"What do you want from me?"

"Stop!"

"I spent thirty years with a man who'd rather leave home and be with her. I was so easy to let go."

"Okay, enough."

"What does she have I didn't have? I don't get it."

"Nothing. Facebook isn't real life."

"Isn't it?"

"I'm not doing this with you."

"Doing what?"

"Do you get where you are?"

"Without a clue."

"You have clues, open your eyes and look at them."

"It was thirty years of my life. He got everything I could give, and he walks away after I beg for us to get help."

"He's not worth it, honey. He's where he belongs with people he'd rather be around."

"Three children, a naval career and the moves. It didn't stick to him."

"He's not worth it anymore."

"Have you seen her?"

"Leave her out of this. She has nothing to do with it."

"Really? I don't think so."

"Okay, yeah, I've seen her, nothing special."

"Why?"

"She has nothing to do with this! He made the choice to pursue the relationship."

"I knew it before it happened."

"What good is it to think about it?"

"I want answers."

"He left, and he's with his kind. That's your answer. Don't blame her, she only knows what he tells her."

"Pisses me off she puts all that shit on Facebook. The kids see it."

"I'm not surprised she's doing it. Stop looking at it."

"I can't."

"You need to."

"I was willing to go with him to South Dakota. I even showed him property in the hills, right outside Hill City, but he was adamant about not going there. It was me, not South Dakota."

"You don't belong there."

"I wanted us to work."

"How many more times would you turn yourself inside out for him?"

"What do you mean?"

"You tried to be what he wanted you to be, but you couldn't please him."

"Sometimes, I think I could have been any woman."

Silence.

"We talked about retirement, where we'd go, spending time with the kids, eventually the grandkids."

"Talk is cheap. How did he treat you, even with all the talk?"

"The same as he always did."

"You deserve better."

"Doesn't matter now anyway. In a fit I told him he should have been with someone from there and he agreed, and now, he has her."

"You don't need to think about love right now."

Silence

"How about living?"

"I can't eat, living is a stretch at this point."

"My sister knows how to live. It's been a while, but she knows how, it's in there."

"I do live."

"You exist."

"So, what?"

"You're better than that. How long before you move forward?"

"Nothing makes sense."

"It will. Time for you to live."

"We went boating with the children to Yorktown on the Fourth, the summer he came back to Virginia to watch the fireworks from the water. It was crowded with boats, and when the display was through, all those boats headed back toward the Poquoson River. The water was rough for us because bigger boats sped past us, leaving a big wake. I was up front with him, holding onto the windshield when we hit one of those waves. I fell into him…"

"And?"

"I fell into him and he shoved me away and said, 'Get the fuck away from me.'"

"Don't tell me any more."

"I've lived life in a bubble for so long I can't imagine how else to live without him."

"Do you remember how you were before? I do. Where is she?"

"I don't."

"I remember the woman who built a deck for him while he was at sea."

"My lesson on how to use a hammer. I forgot about that."

"I didn't. Who the hell does that?"

"I went through boxes of nails. Had I known better, I would have used a drill and screws."

"Whatever, most women don't build decks for their husbands."

"I couldn't wait to see his expression when he came home. All he talked about was having a deck and a lounge chair. I worked every day after work until it was done. When he got home, he was in such a rush to go to South Dakota, he didn't spend any time on it. He left for sea again, and by the time he got home from that deployment, it was time to move. He didn't use it."

"What was his reaction?"

"Surprise. He walked on it and looked at my work. It wasn't perfect, but I was pleased with it."

"You built it alone! Who does that? Where is that woman?"

"I don't know. I don't trust myself."

"Why?"

"Really? Why? Look at my track record. I don't see clearly."

"You can learn."

"I lost my footing with the divorce, and if I was strong, I'm not now, not today, and I don't know how to manage."

"You need help."

"I have a contact."

"Have you called?'

"Not yet."

"What are you waiting for?"

"To hit bottom."

"You're there."

"Am I?"

"Who is this contact?"

"She specializes in healing through touch. She works with my energy to bring balance. I think this will be the best way to get help."

"You need to make an appointment."

"I do."

"When are you calling?"

"Next week."

"Tomorrow."

"That bad?"

"Bad enough."

"What if…"

"No what ifs, understood?"

"I'll call tomorrow and set it up."

"Good. I'll call you tomorrow."

"Okay."

"Sissy?"

"What?"

"I love you. Don't ever forget and think of all the people in your life who are supporting you."

"I will. Thank you, Sis."

5
Self-Care

The room is dimly lit, decorated with her oil paintings, Himalayan salt lamp, large chunk of amethyst, and table. I sit on an oversized recliner while she sits at her desk. Contemplative music plays, and it ripples through the room, softening it. Sharon says it taps into all seven vibrations of my energy field. Her space is clean, and positive energy brushes against me when I walk in, welcoming, loving, keeping me safe.

"I can't move on." I slouch. "What happened? I never thought I'd divorce, never! I'm Catholic! My life was planned!" I hide my face in my hands.

Sharon leans in, her hand graces my arm. "You will get past this. It'll take work, but I promise you will be a new person in a year or so, if you're willing to do the work."

"Work?"

"You can choose to look and understand your journey so far."

"What?"

"Where you've been and why you're here with me now."

"If only…"

Sharon leans back, then rests her hands in her lap. She looks me over before she speaks. "I can't sense joy in you. You don't seek it."

Is this the problem? I lift my leg, cross it, uncross it, and put it down.

"You don't look for happiness either. Your children bring happiness, but you don't look any further for it."

"I want to run away just like he did."

"You can do that. Your guides think a move is a good idea. Give it time."

"Guides?"

She nods.

"My guardian angels?"

"Yes, you have two."

"Really?'

"Yes, really."

"I feel like I seek happiness."

Sharon smiles. "Do you love yourself?"

"Is this why he didn't love me?"

Silence.

"Do you know who you are?"

"I think I know who I am." I sit up.

"Who are you?"

"I'm a woman who spent her youth trying to be a good mother and wife. I gave my family everything I had. I wasn't perfect, but I put my heart into it."

"Who are you?"

"Didn't I just tell you?"

"You told me what you've done but not who you are."

"I am a divorced woman, and I am alone. I need to move on."

"These things you mention are circumstances. They aren't you."

"I give up. Who am I?"

Sharon laughs. "You need to find that out for yourself."

"How?"

"Journey within."

"Within?"

"Yes."

"Are you going with me?"

"To an extent. You need to take the lead, and I will help your body."

"What does that look like?"

"I'll work with your energy system and make sure it flows throughout your body in a healthy way."

"Through touch, right?"

"Yes."

"What will I find within?"

"You."

"How will I know me?"

"You'll come to an understanding of what you need to live in harmony with this world."

"I don't get it."

"What makes you happy? What brings Peace? What brings balance to your life?"

Silence.

"There aren't any definitive answers. We are in flux most of the time, so the best we can do is live each day from the heart and stay connected to the Divine."

"The Divine?"

"Yes, the Divine within and the Divine without."

"Do you mean that still, quiet voice I can't hear anymore?"

Sharon sits up straight. "Yes, the Divine within."

"Is the divine the same as the Holy Spirit?"

"Yes."

"And the Divine without?"

"The Creator, the Good, God."

"I haven't felt either in a long while."

"You will, in time. The Divine lives within, right now, and God is all around."

"Mine headed for cover."

"What?"

"The Divine within, for protection."

"From whom?"

"I don't know, maybe me. I'm a hot mess, Sharon."

"When you open yourself up and are ready to experience it, you'll feel it again and things will be better for you. You'll see yourself."

I shake my head. "Catholics speak of the Holy Spirit which dwells inside, but it needs to be welcomed. I remember being filled with it when I received the sacrament of Confirmation."

"There is so much to look at and try to understand. I encourage you to allow yourself to look beyond what you know."

"What happens once I know who I am?"

"When you know who you are, you will know your bliss."

"I haven't heard this word in years."

"I understand."

"I don't, Sharon."

"Was he willing to make it work?"

"Only on his terms, and this time I said no. He didn't fight for our marriage. Apart but married or apart for always, it didn't matter to him."

"Not an easy thing to realize."

"I took care of him as best I could, but in the end, I couldn't. He was gone in body and in his head. His actions and words told me everything I needed to do. He didn't want me or our life anymore, but he didn't have the courage to get out. It was up to me."

"So then?"

"So, I did what I always did when he was stuck. I took care of him by taking care of business. I got a lawyer and began the process."

"I see."

"My family isn't whole anymore. How do I manage holidays and our future grandchildren? How do I relate to the children, especially now with a new woman in the picture?"

"You don't need answers to these questions; take it as it comes. What matters is you keep the communication open between yourself and your kids. Be honest, let them see you experience the loss. You don't have to be strong all the time. You need to respond to all of this, not react."

"Reacting is natural."

"It is." Sharon pauses. "It's part of our nature to react to events in our lives, but it is healthier to do so from a position of emotional strength."

"When I am emotionally strong, what happens?"

"You respond to life because you are grounded in your truth. Nothing can disrupt your bliss once you are grounded in your truth."

"And where is my truth?"

"It is within."

"It is within, yet I can't find it."

"You will, in time."

"Will I? It's hard to see anything right now."

Sharon grins. "He set you free."

Silence.

She leans in. "He set you free."

"I didn't ask for freedom. I want to be enough just as I am."

"Good. Let's get you on the table."

I pause as I get up. "Why don't you paint anymore?"

"I paint souls now."

Nestled in, she begins. "Mother, Father, God, heavenly creator, we ask the connection be made, and as we connect, we invite and invoke the angels and guides and masters to be in this place in this time. I ask that I be used in the purest form and this be done for the good of all. In Christ's name, we pray." Sharon finishes the invocation and chimes her bells.

I lie there while she whispers, "Take a deep breath… exhale, empty yourself… be in this moment." Her hands are just above my head, but I feel them as if they are on it.

She continues, "Imagine yourself now, someplace you love… find the light, see the light, see it now and let it fill you up… feel its warmth." Her voice fades. As she tends to my body, I look for the light. *Someplace I love… someplace I love… Cape Cod, my summer home.* The wavy music leads me back… back… back… back… *Wellfleet.*

On top of a towering dune just after sunrise, the ocean sweeps the seashore; its melody calms and captivates me as it clears the beach of starfish that took respite from the water at low tide. Hermit crabs dodge the sweeping motion, scurrying in and around the water, and some bury themselves in the wet, cool sand of the morning coastline. Wiggling my bottom left to right to make a seat of sand, I inhale deeply, holding the air in for a count of ten, raising my arms above my head, back straight, eyes closed. I exhale the cleansing breath through my mouth and open my eyes as my arms come to rest in first mudra. I gaze at the ocean, my ocean, the ocean of my youth.

Spanning the horizon, they are there in the distance, flapping about, mere flickers in the sky, close to the surface of the water, as if they are riding the crest of a wave. The sun stretches: yellows, oranges and reds spread themselves out across the sky and my eyes feast on them. She is within reach this time of day. Her radiance is slow to wake up, so I raise my arm, lean forward, open my hand, splay my fingers and reach for her. I try to harness her light and draw it in because I want her to fill me up, but she does not relinquish her luminescence. Using both arms, I reach again, straining myself, but I am too weak to take it. She fades from my mind, and she takes her warmth and colors with her.

I am in a dark place now, but there is enough light to see a figure in the distance, and he comes toward me. It is him, and he is within reach before he stops. We are connected by a light that emanates from our navels. Our eyes meet, and we say nothing before he turns and walks away from me, stretching the light between us, further and further, yet it doesn't snap. We stay connected.

"There you go—walking away, always walking away from me!"

She lays her hands on me as if she is going to massage my body, but she doesn't knead muscles. Her touch is gentle, but deliberate. Both hands survey my body from the top of a limb to its bottom, sometimes quickly, sometimes slowly. She rakes my chest and makes swirls on it without pressure. With her fingertips on my head, she impresses them there before releasing them, often making swirls on my crown too. She does the same with the soles of my feet. Between touches, she rubs her palms together, and she continues until my auric field is clear. Then, she suspends her hands above my torso, palms down, to determine energy flow between the chakras, and she measures my auric field by placing one hand on my shoulder and the other on my hip. She alternates her hands to measure both sides of my body. When she achieves balance in the front, I turn over and she begins the process again.

My sessions with Sharon follow this process, and I leave her office after each subsequent visit securely untethered, as if some force prevents me from being at the mercy of the wind that blows through my being. I am still unsettled and clearly not at peace, but my awareness of where I am comforts and motivates me to do the work. I stand before the mirror, and though I keep one eye closed as I look and the other struggles to focus, I recognize that I am *that* woman: divorced mid-life, one who finds herself in a space she never entertained. I need to pick up the remnants of my life's work and create a new tapestry, one emboldened by the colors of *my* life and blended with the remnants of my married life, but this time, the tapestry needs to be properly tamped.

I hire a contractor to redesign the master bathroom because I need a sanctuary. For years, I see a bathtub in a space that the previous owner used for her dressing and makeup area. The tub is large and deep enough to lounge in without bending my knees. Around it is earth colored stone, enough to build shelving on three sides to hold candles, plants, and a cairn I make from river rock I harvested in western Virginia. It is intended to help bring order, harmony, and balance to the chaos within. Pictures of my garden adorn the walls. I have the shower retiled and its floor covered in river stones to extend the motif from the bathing area. An old ice chest is repurposed as a sink, and an above the counter sink is installed with a faucet that allows water to cascade from it into the bowl. The contractor asks, "What are you looking for?" I smile. "Zen."

I spend winter soaking by candlelight, sipping herbal remedies and tapping. Using acupressure, accountability, and affirmations, tapping supports balance and alleviates emotional pain. I practice it to help me work through fear and scarcity, for fortitude and hope and prosperity. Forgiveness? Well, this is particularly difficult for me on so many levels, but I try… I try hard to forgive him first.

I begin as I tap the side of my palm. *Even though I am resisting forgiveness,*

I choose to love and accept myself. Mr. Yates begins, "There is one I am having a hard time to forgive. I refuse to forgive, and to some extent, this means I am refusing to forgive myself." I am supposed to repeat his words, but I stop. "This isn't about me," I say to him on YouTube. "It's about forgiving him." Mr. Yates taps his forehead and so do I. I repeat his words. "I choose to forgive." I tap my cheekbone. "All this resistance... if I choose to forgive, it will happen again. But by not forgiving, I stop myself from healing." I tap under my arm and recite these words to clear the thought that I accept the nastiness, dismissiveness, and disrespect if I forgive. This takes effort and I find myself tapping with force. Mr. Yates continues, and I follow. "I'm clearing it out, clearing it out at a cellular level because clearing it out doesn't mean I am condoning his actions, approving of his actions or forgetting, but when I forgive, I choose to stop suffering."

Staying focused, I tap deliberately and more quickly. My palm taps my chest. "I choose to take responsibility for how I feel, and I choose to feel good. I am forgiving him for my own benefit. I may never know if it makes a difference to him or not, but by not forgiving him, I'm not putting him in a cage, I am putting myself in one." I do not want to let go; I want to hold on to indignation as though it is a medal of honor, a pass given because of my experiences with him, but I keep going. Tapping my temple, I say, "I choose to forgive... forgiveness to myself and him; and I am worthy of that and so is he. I am setting myself free with forgiveness, in body, mind and soul."

I take a deep breath, exhale, and rest. Introspection is a new concept I find agreeable and tapping facilitates my efforts to go deeply, so I practice this technique sometimes three times a day.

In the evenings, I meditate while I bathe since water enhances the power of meditation, and as I succumb to the warm water, my body relaxes and releases toxins. I set the mood with music, choosing instrumentals with subtle tones. Native American flute music is particularly conducive to meditation, though I am not sure why. Its cadence enters me and swirls about my mind like the smoke from a snuffed candle; and it has an aroma, like incense, pleasant and purposeful. The music is a loyal friend to the soul, and it brings me to a higher place and stays with me if I wish. There, I rinse my mind as one rinses a dirty bowl that has sat in the sink for days. Once it is clean, it can be filled, and through meditation, one has the potential to be filled with nothing, which is everything. It is challenging to reach a higher vibration because I am preoccupied with others' perceptions of me, him, her and their life. In other words, this world. It takes months, but I persevere, and I let go for five minutes, then ten, fifteen, thirty. I see the woman I want to be- strong, independent, loving, and not just to those who love me, but to humanity, and yes, that includes him and her. It is about me for the time being, though, and with my energy tuned in, I see the shackles around my chafed ankles, ironclad and faded.

Though bearable, I feel their presence now. Self-imprisoned in my marriage, I desire to release myself, but I do not have the strength. I am married to my marriage, still living the roles of wife and mother and overwhelmed over the meaning of intimacy between a man and a woman.

In a groove, going about the business of life, but not living it, I exist. In those rare moments of nothingness, I petition the light for a way out. It answers, "Shift." Robert Frost comes to me, "Two roads diverged in a wood, and I, I took the one less traveled by, and that has made all the difference," and an outpouring of emotions come to the surface too; and they have no names, are heavy and look like the blobs in lava lamps. They gather like puddles in the yard after a spring rain. On the landscape of my being they are unavoidable, as billboards along the bucolic county roads of Virginia. "I am ready," I say, and two months after the divorce is final, I begin. My first test comes in December when he comes back east for the holiday.

We try to create a semblance of normalcy as we knew it for the sake of the children. The table is set, the schedule is posted on the white board. We play our parts, the children do as well, and then we take our assigned seats, pray, pour wine and converse as if all is as it should be. This reality confuses me, and a blanket of emotions shroud my vision. Drinking wine doesn't help, but I continue to consume with the hope it will clear the fog. It only exacerbates it, though. All my insecurities with their accompanying questions surface, eclipsing further my lack of sight, and by the end of the evening, I follow him to his truck as he excuses himself and says goodbye. He sees me glance at the empty beer cans in the pickup bed, smirks, and lets out a laugh. "Now what?" I ask.

"What do you mean?"

"Her. Have you spoken to the children about her and what she means?"

"No."

"Do you plan to? How do we introduce her?"

"Whatever." He shrugs. "You need to move on. It's all done. Time to move on." He starts up the truck and turns it around.

I wave and hold my hands up. He rolls down his window. "What?"

"Just a minute, I'll be right back." I run in and grab the tin off the counter, bring it outside and hand it to him through the window. "I made these for Mom. Please make sure she gets them." I step back, he rolls up the window and drives away.

For the next several days my body is on high alert, reacting to anything that crosses its path. I twitch and do not want to be touched; I lack the ability to concentrate for any length of time and a general malaise reigns; and the growth I thought I achieved in the preceding months under Sharon's guidance is soured like milk past its expiration date. Sitting with my adult children is uneasy, and they know something is upsetting me, and I do not want to tell them, but finally I do, though I have no clue what it is, and I explain the experience as a tremor one might feel after an earthquake. I have only one recourse: Sharon. She will understand; she will help me navigate through the assault on my energy field.

"I had to come, something's not right."

"What happened?" Sharon offers me water.

"He came over for Christmas."

"Why?"

"The children."

"How did it go?"

"He was polite. He knocked on the door before he came in, and we were civil. But it got weird, especially at dinnertime. It was like we weren't divorced. We fell into roles like it was nothing, me the submissive wife wanting peace, him the man of the house. Had you walked in our dining room on Christmas Eve, you'd have thought we were an intact family celebrating the holiday together."

"How did you feel?"

"Freaked me out. I haven't been right since. I told the kids this morning that I had to see you. Something is wrong."

"You brought her back."

"Her?"

"The wife. You aren't comfortable with her anymore. We need to send her to the light."

"How?"

"Do you give me permission to send her?"

"Yes."

"Let's pray. Mother, Father, God, we ask your angels to come and escort Wife now so that we dissolve the cord of connection." Sharon is still before she nods. "The angels are escorting her to the light, to the next dimensional plane to be healed in wholeness and completeness." She is quiet for a few seconds. "Wife is in the first plane, now second, third…" Sharon is still. "She's in the light, amen."

"Amen. Why did I do this?"

"What do you mean?"

"Why did I play along as if nothing happened?"

"You did what was expected of you."

"I did?"

"You filled a role for your family as you've always done."

"I'm not even aware of my actions. I can't do this again."

"You won't. Wife is in the light now and you see what happened."

"I thought I could handle it, but I couldn't."

"What else happened?"

"I tried to reach him by accepting his new life and lover. I spoke with him outside before he left. Part of me didn't want him to leave."

"Was he receptive?"

"I was emotional, and he wasn't. He told me it was time to let go and move on. I stared at him as he spoke. There wasn't any emotion, nothing. He pulled away, taking a piece of me with him. Is this strange?"

"You say you always feel connected to him."

"I can't go on like this."

"Let's go to the table." Sharon gets up and motions me to follow. Her touch brings balance to my body and restores my energy system, and I resolve to take better care of myself and avoid situations that disrupt my peace until I am stronger. In the interim, I continue to shift to a better place.

Music is the vehicle that supports me as I struggle through it. Longing for an embrace from God, I sing along with George Harrison, "Give me light, give me life, keep me free from birth, give me hope, help me cope with this heavy load, trying to touch and reach you with heart and soul, ohmmmmmm... my Lord... please take hold of my hand that I might understand..." Carlos Santana manipulates me like a snake charmer, and my body moves to his steel guitar. Over and over and long into the night he and I are together. He motivates me to work on myself, to take the time to care for my body and my appearance, reminding me as I sway to *Smooth*, "You're my reason for reason, the step in my groove... and it's just like the ocean under the moon, that's the same emotion as I get from you. You've got the kind of lovin that can be so smooth..." Perhaps it is serendipitous or divine intervention, but whatever it is, I need it. The Moody Blues come through Hampton Roads to perform at The Ferguson Center, and I buy a center row ticket.

I tune in to the large crowd of strangers who become an intimate group of individuals about to share an encounter and see a familiar pattern. Most of us are over fifty and from many walks of life. I recognize old hippies. Many wear dated concert t-shirts. "He loves them as much as I do," a grandfather says to another about his grandson who stands at his side.

I take my seat between two couples, exchange greetings, and settle in. The theater lights dim, the stage lights brighten, casting shades of blues that fill the stage and the backdrop. The colors are blurred; they create a cosmic, transcendental ambience that orients us. Justin Haywood and John

Lodge come on stage, and there is a tremendous uproar of applause. Their presence is impressive, and when they begin playing, it is exhilarating; it is hard to believe both men are in their seventies because their youthfulness supersedes their ages.

Closing my eyes, I go to that place. "So take your share of the gifts that are there, they all belong to you… we all begin anew once more… we all begin anew… let's lose our way, go completely astray and find ourselves again," they sing. My shoulders bob to the beat of the drum. It is time to shift. "Cause out on the ocean of life my love, there's so many storms we must rise above… can you hear the spirit calling as it's carried across the waves? You're already falling, it's calling you back to face the music and the song that is coming through… make a promise, take a vow, and trust your feelings, it's easy now. Understand the voice within and feel a change already beginning." Peace joins me at intermission.

"Have you seen them a lot?" the gentlemen to my left asks.

"This is my first time."

"I follow them wherever I can. I saw them in Richmond last night. I even went to England to see them when my daughter was there."

"You're a devoted fan." I reseat myself to face him.

"They helped me through a rough time, and I will always be grateful to them."

"I can relate."

"Oh? My rough time was my divorce."

"Mine too."

"Are you on the other side?"

"Not yet, but I'm working to get there."

"How long?"

"I've been divorced five months."

"Yes, you have a way to go yet. Is he with someone else?"

"Yes. It didn't take long."

"I remember. It's a blow, but recoverable."

"We'll see."

"How long have you listened to them?"

"Since I was a girl."

"I was a teenager when they came on the scene."

"Their words speak to me."

"I know." He smiles. "The words eased my sorrow. It took a long while to get through it, but I did. There is life on the other side."

"Thank you, I appreciate your kindness, and I hope so. That's what I'm looking forward to."

"I think you'll be all right." The gentleman pauses and considers my eyes. "Yes, I'm sure of it."

6

Victim

Suspended animation (noun): "The temporary cessation of most vital functions without death, as in a dormant seed or hibernating animal." This is me, just there, going through the motions, smiling-not really.

There is no rest. Thoughts, lots of thoughts. Why the angst? Why the turmoil? The squatters are still there, vying for a piece of me! There is no balance. My legs shake, my hands are clenched, and my head tilts side to side as though *I* am now the prize fighter just before the bout, but they continue to battle each other. I am their host and am expected to move on, to get over it, or as Mother suggests, "bury it deep and turn to God".

Looking around, I see it. People turn the page, eager for chapter two; hopefully, the plot twist will bring a happy ending. The exception, not the rule, I need to study the page before I turn it. What inferences can be made? What does the dialogue reveal about the characters I did not notice in the narrative? My husband made a seamless transition into a new life, telling me, "*That* life is over. I don't think about it anymore." Shit! In my scarier moments, I choose my cave where it is dark, but there is no rest.

"It is you," a voice says. "You did this." *Me?* "Look at you! What happened to your trim figure? Remember the days you wore a string bikini? You were desirable then. Now, you look matronly and if I were you, I wouldn't wear a bathing suit ever!" *Please! Don't go there.* "She's very thin… nothing to her, in fact, and you know how he likes that." *I know I let myself go, don't rub it in… it's too much.* "And then there's your hair? Why are you growing it out like that?" *I like it.* "It's gray! Remember he said you looked old like that?" "Besides, you're a bore, always the designated driver, the responsible one, the show pony. And don't forget one of his names for you… Church Lady." *Stop!* "Not very sexy, right? Maybe you were too much this way?" *I was there for him! Always! Through the absences, the drinking, the accusations, and the mistrust… and the fucking names! And I did it alone because it's what he wanted. I loved him!*

"How are you?" Sharon asks.

"Not good."

"What has happened since last week?"

Silence.

"What is it?"

"I'm under attack."

"From whom?"

"The thing with no name."

"What do you see?"

"It's hard to see anything or understand what I experienced over this summer. Last summer was bad enough! I was married for thirty years, and he picks up a new life as if our life meant nothing. I tried to be a good wife. I took care of the children, the house, and the bills so he could be successful. I wanted him happy. I didn't deny him when he wanted something, and all those somethings were left behind. They weren't enough and I wasn't either. Now he's off in South Dakota with her, and she posts it all on Facebook. Did I miss something?"

"Are you a victim?"

"No! He said the same thing to me. I'm nobody's victim!"

"Good, because it sounded as if…"

"What do you mean?" A wave of heat oscillates throughout my body.

"You can choose to be a victim."

"Sometimes people are victims through no fault of our own."

"Are they?"

"I think so."

"How?"

"I didn't expect to be dismissed and disrespected in my marriage."

"You allowed it."

"I didn't invite it."

"You allowed it."

"I didn't want discord."

"You had it anyway."

"What was I supposed to do?"

"It's not my place to tell you what you should have done. I'm pointing out what happened in your marriage."

"It doesn't matter now. He rejected me."

"Watch your words."

"Really? I chose this?"

"I think you know what you did." Sharon looks at me and then to her notes. We are quiet. Inhaling, I lift my shoulders as high as they will go while flexing them against my neck; I hold my breath and listen to the white noise in my head. As I exhale, they fall back into place. I discern activity within. "I was hopeful," I begin. "I wanted my babies to have what I didn't have, a mom *and* a dad, so they'd grow up feeling whole and secure. That's what fathers do for their children. He was a good provider and responsible, and we knew how to parent; and although I raised the children, he steered our course. I was the boat, and he was the rudder. It was smooth sailing for them, so I thought he and I could make it. I wanted to give the children a happy marriage, more than anything else, and I was willing to take anything for that, so I took it, trying to fix it along the way."

"No fault in hoping for a good marriage."

"What kind of woman loves a man who treats her poorly?"

"That's a question you'll need to answer."

Silence.

"Your marriage wasn't healthy."

"What do you mean?"

"There wasn't equity in the relationship."

"What was there?"

"I think you need to tell me."

"I wanted help. I wanted to fix us. I didn't feel sorry for me. I was in, had been for thirty years, and I wanted him in too, for us."

"If you speak like a victim, you are a victim. Victims react, not respond to life." I rest my chin in the palms of my hands as a well of uncontrollable emotion comes toward the surface. Sharon counsels, "You can't fix us either."

"It's not fair! Why does he get to leave and start over? He walked into a new life complete with a lover and friends! Why doesn't he suffer?"

"Anger can be productive, but don't get comfortable with it."

"It's all I have right now."

"I see."

"I thought he loved me."

"Did you ever think his lack of love for you had everything to do with him?"

"No."

"He has his struggles. You saw this, and the life his girlfriend projects on Facebook isn't the story. You need to turn your attention to your journey and leave him to his."

"Easier said than done."

"I encourage you to read and find answers for yourself. I have some sources to get you started."

Silence

"You said you weren't always sure what to expect?"

"I knew what was expected of me. I assumed the rest."

"Assumed?"

"I thought he loved me and wanted to be with me, even with our issues."

"When did you know he didn't?"

"At the end"

"And now?"

"I can't look at myself in the mirror. I see myself, but I look past me, barely acknowledge the reflection, pretty much dismiss it. That's messed up."

"You don't see yet."

"What?"

"Do you love yourself?"

"This isn't about me."

"Who is this about?"

"Him and what he did!"

"He's gone. His behavior doesn't impact you anymore. Let him go."

"I can't."

"Your answers lay inside, and once you understand you are not a victim, all will be revealed."

It is twilight, a period marked with ambiguity, and I am in the garden along with the crepuscular critters who dwell there with my mug in hand. I am exhausted after my counseling session. Anger is temporarily eased but simmering below and poised on the precipice of rationality. Without any thought, I take a step forward into my space.

Neglected while I navigated the tumultuous seas of separation in a lifeboat, the garden is in disarray and desperate to be weeded and nurtured. It has been my haven, and in it I have dawdled, but no more. What comes to mind is the story *The Secret Garden*, and I fixate on mine, fantasizing that amid the overgrowth and ever-present chickweed and henbit, the illustrious canopy of color and fragrance will carry me to a place where I am whole again, physically, emotionally, and spiritually. Fantasies keep me reaching as though they are brass rings on the merry-go-round of life. Reality does not need to be grasped; it is in front of me, sometimes clear, sometimes beguiling.

Enchanting, the garden lures me in. I am its captive, but its song, like the song of the Siren, is empty. Before me lays a mess, an overgrown piece of land abandoned by a once enthusiastic gardener. I cannot smell anything, see texture, and color is washed out.

I schlep about it looking for signs of life anyway, hoping something in it will revive me, perhaps new growth on the gardenia and viburnum. Both suffered through freezing winter temperatures. A feeling harkens me back to my youth and beyond to lives once lived and felt deep within my being, but incomprehensible to me in my current state. I want to reach back; I want to understand, but I am lost, like I was after Daddy died. I bend down to my knees and lower my head to connect to self, but it is futile. There is a barrier between us, and my Eden, once an oasis, is now a desert; God cannot be found anywhere, even among the happy volunteers, her favorite hiding place. Maybe she has left with the birds to find a happier, more serene garden, one that is loved. I glance to my left and find a cigar stub under the forsythia. I pick it up and chuck it into the woodland. "How many more of these did you leave behind?"

The surviving pansies are bowing; their limp stems and forlorn faces of blues, yellows and creams plead with me to quench their thirst. I oblige, offering my apologies. Had I bothered to deadhead them, I would have a flush of new color to look forward to in a couple of weeks. As it is, many have succumbed to the heat. While I water them, my eyes catch a glimpse of Iris virginica; faithful in the garden in years past, its faintly smelling flowers with dainty sepals and erect petals cast a dark lavender spell on the bog garden. Each bloom has a splash of yellow too, and its zigzagging stalk adds vertical interest for this once avid naturalist. Since I did not divide it last season, or the season prior, its blooms are sporadic, and the bog is now overgrown with green foliage. The spell is broken.

Black-eyed Susan winks at me as I pass her on my way to the vegetable garden. She greets all visitors to the butterfly garden and invites them to visit. She is a gracious hostess, and I accept her invitation. It is my favorite spot, filled with fennel, native Echinacea, milkweed, and mint, and it has thrived below one of my bedroom windows for years. Recording its evolution from an immature and managed plot to a naturally occurring ecosystem that hosts birds, bees, snakes, box turtles and butterflies, I watched it from on high; and in its season the bees have their way with my flowers. There are only a few butterflies flittering about the flora this balmy Virginia morning, and it is just as well. I cannot welcome them home, not with any enthusiasm. Black-eyed Susan does my bidding instead.

She thrives on her own. With a laissez-faire quality about her, she sows her seeds freely throughout the garden, taking root wherever she fancies, be it full sun or dappled shade. She even has the tenacity to spring up through cracks in the driveway and sidewalk. Resiliency is her hallmark, like crabbers who navigate the precarious waters of the Chesapeake Bay for a lifetime. She abounds in my garden, thank goodness, and I cannot help but smile. Across from her is a statue of Saint Francis.

He keeps company with bee balm. A stray tendril of Betty Corning is spiraled around his torso, though, and the lovely bell-shaped flowers of this Clematis are appropriate for him because they are reminiscent of church bells whose peal evokes images of heavenly hosts. Francis was called to reform The Church. "Preach the gospel at all times and when necessary, use words," he said. He was a man of the earth, in communion with the energy around us, and he spoke of living simply with it, for there is where God resides. He spoke of suffering too, insisting God speaks to us through it. I identify with Brother Francis; in him, I see me, her, if only I can reach her, but coming to accept suffering takes faith that it will bring goodness. I am not convinced I can suffer, not like Francis, though I feel I have been lately. Is this victimhood? Is the attack within victimhood too? Will you show me the way, Francis? I kneel and weed the bed at the base of the statue. *Start by doing what's necessary, then what's possible, and suddenly, you're doing the impossible.* His words ring in my ears, and I find myself repeating them as if they are a Gregorian chant. "Can you hear me Blessed Mother? I'm sorry, I'm sorry."

A bunny grazing among the clover captures my attention. He nibbles one clover after another, taking all he can, and although I resist the urge to look for meaning in his actions while he forages, I desperately want it to be a sign of something, anything, but his effort is prosaic, like mine: survival motivates us, not poetry.

If you speak like a victim, you are a victim. If you speak like a victim, you are a victim. If you speak like a victim, you are a victim. These words are not soothing; they are a wake-up call, like reveille at dawn. I imagine covering my ears with a pillow, as a sailor the morning after leave in Rio during carnival, to drown it out but it's no use. I cannot go back to sleep. I turn my attention elsewhere, the vegetable garden, but Sharon's words follow me there.

The ground lays fallow for another season, and the chickweed moves in and spreads quickly in the loam. It is impossible to clear out without chemicals, which I refuse to use, but the situation will need to be addressed. It is here, amid the chick weed and sundry other undesirables, I realize the garden and I are similar. We need weeding and new compost before cultivating, and in my moment of insight that pesky, annoying, and unwanted entity, the one with no name, is known. Victim. He rears his ugly head and demands attention. We convene.

I have nothing to say to you.

"I have plenty to say to you."

You are not a friend, you are a predator. I see this now, an imposter really.

"Sharon tell you this?"

I can figure things out for myself.

"Can you? This isn't my experience with you."

That was before...

"Please! There is no before, no after either, just right now, this very second."

So?

"You're engaging me. Truth be told, you want me around."

I get up quickly and go to the house to put the kettle on, not knowing that I am out of chamomile and must choose between lemon and detox. I prefer lemon in the morning, so hesitantly, I plop a detox blend into a mug and pour. Victim sits with me at the kitchen table and starts in.

"Why are you avoiding me?"

We aren't friends!

"You and I are dear friends, several years now, ever since he decided to leave your bed and life."

I remember, and I remember the pain of rejection I didn't deserve.

"That's right, keep going."

Why, why?

"Why indeed!"

I did as he asked, but I couldn't make him happy... so much I let go for him...

so much of myself I buried to try to please him.

"This is great! What an asshole! You deserved so much more!"

Wait, I don't think this is healthy.

"What do you mean? You were a good and loving wife. Have you forgotten?"

No, but…

"You took good care of him, the children and all their lives. You were the glue!"

Yes, but I did all that for love."

"Of course, you did because you are a loving person."

I was, and I deserve better.

"Yes, you do, and you thought later it would be different."

It should have been. I earned a happy ending.

"He didn't appreciate you."

No, he didn't.

"After all you did…"

Yes, after all that!

"You see what I mean now. I am your friend… I am your true friend because I get you."

Yes, but I knew a happy marriage was always a few beers away. His drinking…

"You tolerated it, even after you asked him over and over again to leave it alone."

I wonder now if we could have ever been…

"Don't!"

What?

"Don't think like that! Thirty years! You gave him all you had, and in the end it wasn't enough."

I know.

"He played you! Back and forth, spinning, tip toeing, even in the end. Have you forgotten those eggshells? You should have taken more!"

He knew how to play me.

"He wasn't loyal; he thought only of himself. Have you forgotten the mess? His tools? Everything was left behind."

The money I spent to clear it all out.

"Right! Now you're seeing it."

Why? Why do this to me? No respect!

"Keep going, see? See what he did? You didn't deserve any of this."

It's over now. I'm getting stronger. I don't need to go back. I'm moving forward.

"Are you?"

Am I what?

"Moving forward?"

I think so

"If you were moving forward, I wouldn't be here."

Stop!

"Truth is you don't need to move forward. Everything you feel about this whole mess is valid. He did this to you!"

Please. I'm tired of this. I get up and walk to the back room for air. Restless, I pace back and forth in the empty space. I fall onto the beanbag chair, hoping its tendency to surround one would bring a sense of security, but it is confining, and I roll off it and onto the floor. Berber carpet is rough, not at all conducive to anything except heavy foot traffic, so I get up and go back to my tea and Victim.

"Yes, sit down… you deserve to."

If you speak like a victim, you are a victim… if you speak like a victim, you are a victim.

"Really? When have you spoken like a victim? When? You're a bystander, since childhood, always watching, taking it all in, but never taking control."

Where are you going with this?

"You can't help it. You've never been able to help it."

Help? Help what?

"Who supported you as a child? Your beloved father dies and the adults in your life are worthless! No one supported you. You were left alone to cope with the impossible. Have you forgotten the loneliness? The tears? The anguish in the pit of your stomach?"

What are you talking about? This is about my marriage and him!

"This is true. He was a shit to you. We can talk about him all you want."

I don't know why you'd bring up the past.

"Well, it's the only way for you to understand our relationship."

I wouldn't call this a relationship.

"I definitely would, and I hope it continues for a long time."

I didn't ask for your friendship.

"You did, and I intend to be a loyal friend."

Look, I don't have any answers. Shit, I don't even know how to ask questions yet. What I know is Sharon's words have meaning for me and the life I want to lead. I hate them too, but I can't embrace the alternative.

"Why? There are thousands upon thousands of people out there who understand where you've been. They'll support you."

I don't want their support. This doesn't feel right, not anymore.

"You can't mean it!"

I've allowed you in, but you need to leave.

"I won't go without a fight."

I know. I get up.

"Where are you going?"

For a walk… and thank you.

"For what?"

For being you

"Does this mean you've reconsidered?"

It means you've opened my eyes and I see what I don't want to be, and you are right, I need to look back through a child's eyes, mine.

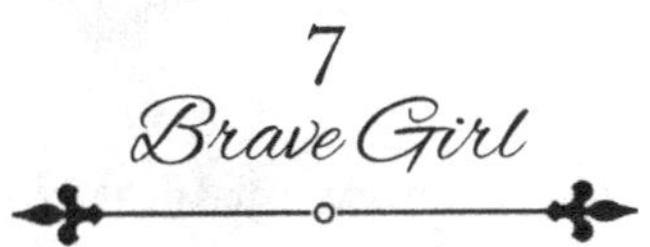

7

Brave Girl

The best thing about third grade is recess. When the bell rings, I run faster than the whole class to the playground and get to the swings before they do. I get one of the end swings and these are better than the others because you only have one person next to you, and this is better because you're free and no one talks to you and you can swing like you want and think like you want to.

I'm thinking a lot about Daddy today. He has cancer, but not for a long time. I told my teacher, Miss Taylor, at the beginning of the year and she put her arm around me and said she got it. How come she gets it? I don't. I think Mrs. Kennedy knows too, but I'm not sure. She's my French teacher, and I only see her three times a week, and she only speaks French to me. *Petite fille, tu es*, something, something *pour* something. I know a lot of words, but I don't know everything. She has a real big mouth like the ones you see in cartoons on Saturdays, and when she opens it, she moves her lips real fast and real slow to show me how to say words. I'm glad they know. I don't feel alone so much.

I'm not sure when the cancer came. He was sick before this and what he had has a long name that begins with a C. Hold on… I know the word, I know it! Colostomy! Anyway, Daddy has to wear a bag near his belly button, and he goes to the bathroom in it. It's yucky to watch him change it, but he's my daddy so it's okay. After he flushes the toilet I ask, "Is it time to shave?" He says, "Yes," and I move closer to him, sitting on the bathroom rug at his feet.

"Sing, Daddy!"

"Oh, the monkey wrapped his tail around the flagpole to see his…" He stops and laughs.

"Keep going!"

He goes to the hospital a lot now, most of the time in winter, and we have a ton of snow this year. I can't see out the kitchen windows after one storm, and my brother has to shovel through it and make a path for the ambulance bed. It takes all morning for him to do it, but he works hard and doesn't get mad, and in the afternoon, the bed gets through. Most of the time he is a dink, but not when he's like this, and I think maybe we can be friends and he won't tease and be mean to me anymore. It hurts when he hits me, and I don't like it when he calls me 'dog' all the time. Mom says Daddy is getting treatment, but I'm not sure what this means. He goes back and forth to the hospital more than he goes to work right now. First in a car, but now in the ambulance. At least the snow is all gone and it's warmer outside. No one tells me why, but I think it's a faster ride in the ambulance. The doctors say they can fix him so they want to get it done, and then Daddy can get back to work and everything will be the same again.

The hospital is gross. It smells like the iodine I use for scrapes. The floors are dirty yellow with brown specks, and the walls are green like the Necco wafer. The people there are very sick, sicker than Daddy, and I tiptoe without talking because I don't want to wake them up. Daddy's room is small, and everything is white except the floor; it's like the other floor outside. He lies there sorta smiling, but it looks like it's hard to do. He can't move around a lot because he has a tube in his arm. "Hi, Daddy." He turns to look at me, his pajama top open. "What happened?"

The scar looks like a big cross, and it covers his chest. "I had something taken out of me."

I stare at it. "Does it hurt?"

"Not too much."

I swing and going back and forth makes it easy. The scar is better but still scary, and I think about Jesus every time I look at it, and I wonder if Daddy is like Jesus because he suffers. My catechism teacher tells me Jesus died for me because he loves me. Daddy can't think this, can he? Maybe our guardian angels can talk to each other and I can find out what to do so Daddy doesn't suffer anymore. He doesn't have to show me he loves me. I know he does.

He's nice to me, plays with me and takes me places, and he lets me sit on his lap at night when he watches the news. All that's on is the war and Daddy holds me close when the man talks about the boys dying over there, and he stares at the TV, and he's not happy or sad. It's like he's someplace else just for a second, and I remember his uniform from the war he was in, but he can't miss war, can he? The pictures on TV are sad. The boys are crying and so many are hurt, and other boys put cigarettes in their mouths and then light them like they're medicine or something. They look scared when they are shooting, but I don't know who they're shooting at. Commercials make Daddy feel better, especially the shaving cream one with the football player and the pretty girls. He doesn't hold me so close then, but he doesn't watch the news anymore. He doesn't do anything except stay in bed and be sick.

I hear him coughing, and I count them… one, two, three, four… twenty, twenty-one… most of the night. Sometimes he gets up and his slippers slide across the carpet, and I think about sparks coming out of them like my brother's Godzilla toy. He coughs so much and so hard, and it is so scary I wrap myself in my sheet and try to cover my ears with it. My hands hurt because I press them against my head hard, and I wonder how much it hurts to cough so much. I remember I had one at Christmas and my chest burned, and I didn't cough nearly as hard as he does. It must be like a fire inside him. Then Daddy moans too, and I get butterflies, but not the good butterflies like when you are on a fun ride at the carnival. These are the bad butterflies, like the time I got them when I cut my leg real bad and blood gushed out.

I can swing higher than anyone in my class, even better than the boys. Miss Taylor worries I'm going too high. "Be careful!" She yells from the blacktop, and I yell back, "I like going high!" Ever since I told her about Daddy, she makes sure I'm okay. She always smiles at me when I walk in and she asks about him. I tell her what I can but there is so much I don't get, and no one explains it to me because they are busy taking care of him. But I try and Miss Taylor doesn't mind I can't answer her questions. She keeps smiling and pats my back and says, "Why don't you get to your seat, it's time to get started." I'm a good girl for her and I skip to my seat, but by lunch, I'm not so good and I wish I was.

I don't want to do my schoolwork because I feel yucky, but I don't know why, and it makes me sad. I always get my work done and I try to be the first one too because I want to be the best in the class. School is way easy and besides, I like it. I'm in the highest reading and math groups. We're learning to read French right now, and I love the way the words sound and the way my tongue works when I say them. They are pretty and they make a song when you say them right. Mrs. Kennedy shows us a map of France and it looks like a side view of a man and I laugh when I see it. "Lola?" Mrs. Kennedy says. *"Ca va?"* *"Oui Madame."* I cover my mouth with my hands. Maybe one day I'll go there and talk with all the French people. That would be fun! Good thing I have Mrs. Kennedy. She is a really good teacher. I'm afraid I'm going to be moved out of the high groups if I don't work, and I want to work but I'm stuck, like I'm in quicksand and I don't want to think about this because it's very scary. It's hard to get out of quicksand, so I don't think about it. I doodle instead.

No one taught me how to do it, and it's not hard to do. Just let your brain go, and with your pencil, draw what you're thinking about. I draw a lot of flowers, and they become gardens, and then, I decorate them like Christmas. I use colored pencils to do that. Miss Taylor tells me my doodles are very good, and then she asks me to do my work, but I still don't want to.

"Can I keep doing it?" I ask.

She says, "Why don't you make a card for your father. You can write a short letter to him using lined paper. You know where it is. Start with 'Dear Daddy,' and don't forget the comma like we learned. You can tell him how much you love him and hope he is better soon. Once you're finished, we'll put the paper on top of a piece of colored paper—"

"Purple?"

"Any color you want. We'll put your letter on the purple paper and then fold it in half to make the card."

"Can I doodle on the cover?"

"Yes, if you want, okay?"

"Okay."

Still, I swing, and today, higher than ever. It scares me a little because the chain clinks and I bounce. Kenneth sees and pumps harder.

"You can't catch me!" I yell.

"Yes I can!"

"Just try then!"

Boys think they're better than girls with outdoor stuff. They're not, but they get all the chances because they get to play football and baseball and everything else. We can't because we're girls. How stupid is this! We're supposed to be "sugar and spice and everything nice." Well, I like sugar but it's sticky, and I like some spices, the kinds at Christmas but I don't get this saying at all. I like to play hard and run fast, and it feels good to get sweaty like I did something. I can sit still if I have to, but why do I have to all the time? And I'm not going to! I have recess to be better, and when Kenneth swings, I do too, as hard as I can. Daddy said to Mom, "She is an athlete, if only she was a boy." I love Daddy, so I try to be a boy, the best boy, for him. If I could change my name, it would be Tommy, but I can't do that. Even when I try, Mom ignores me, and my brother laughs at me.

"You're a girl, you can't do what boys do!"

"You're a dink weed," I say. "I'm better than you at running, and I'm tougher too!"

"I can still hurt you."

"I hate you!"

"When you grow up, you're going to marry someone just like me!"

"No! I'm not!"

The bell rings, but I keep swinging until the chain clinks again and then I jump! The ground is hard and I scrape my knees. Mom is going to be mad; she always gets mad about my knees. She says when I come in the kitchen door, "When are going to have presentable knees?!" I can't answer her question. All I can do is bring them together, spit on my fingers and wipe them fast. "Get up to the tub and scrub them," she says. "And take your clothes off here, I don't want you traipsing through the house in them." She says, "Why are you such a tomboy!?" I can hide my knees from Mom, and even though they burn, I wipe the gravel out of the scrapes and get in line with my class.

I have my reading book open and a worksheet in front of me. Miss Taylor says, "The office called for you."

"Am I in trouble?"

In the hallway I turn around, and Miss Taylor is standing outside the door. Her hand is covering her mouth. The last time she did this was when Seth was hit by a car. He broke his legs and was in a cast forever. He had a neat wheelchair though, and sometimes we pushed him around on the blacktop during recess. As I run my hand along the hallway wall, my head thinks a lot. *Maybe everyone knows I took Linda's purse from the coat room! I gave it back the next day! I hung it where it was, so it doesn't matter, right!? What am I going to do!? I'm going to get in so much trouble if Mom finds out! And no one will like me either!* "Ouch!" I stop and look at the tip of my finger. Something sharp on the wall pricks it.

"Your mother wants you home."

Silence.

"Get your things and go home," Mrs. Queander says.

"Now?"

"Yes, now. She wants you to walk home."

Miss Taylor hugs me before she opens the door. "See you tomorrow," I say. She doesn't say anything back.

I pick up a fallen chestnut from underneath the gigantic tree just before the path. I peel the shell off as fast as I can, which isn't very fast because it's hard to do. I know there's a chestnut inside, but I don't know how big it is and this makes peeling it exciting, like opening Christmas and birthday presents. The nut is pretty big, but not the biggest I've had before. It sits in the palm of my hand and I rub it with my fingers until I see my favorite flowers.

Mom teaches me about daffodils, and we plant them in her garden. She laughs and tells me about the times I picked them "bulb and all" and brought them to her. They are on the sides of the path, bunches and bunches of yellow. I drop the chestnut, leave the path, and pick a clump for Daddy. I skip the rest of the way. My hair is in my eyes, my knee socks are around my ankles, my skirt is crooked, and I scrape the toes of my patent leather shoes a couple of times. Oops! I don't care because it is warm and sunny and all around me is yellow.

I march down the hill to my house holding the daffodils like they are a baton and I'm in the Patriots' Day parade. It's downtown in the month of April, and I want to be in it next year. Straight and tall, looking out front with people clapping their hands and smiling at me, I pay attention and pretend I'm a twirler. One time a girl dropped her baton in the middle of the parade, and she had to jump out of line and then back in again. I never want that to happen to me! Mom says I can take lessons in the fall. For now, the flowers will have to do, and I keep marching, one, two, three, four, one, two, three, four. Daddy was in the parade last year because he's in the Elks Club. He sat on the back of a red car without a top and waved to the crowd. He threw candy to us kids.

I get to my back yard and halt... one, two. Auntie is there leaning against the old oak tree smoking a cigarette. She doesn't come to my house a lot, and I don't know why, something about living too far away, but I'm happy to see her because she's nice to me. The tree is the biggest one in the yard and my favorite, home base for kickball and baseball, and it's where Daddy stands and teaches me.

She's looking up at the sky like I do, and she looks like she's thinking about it real hard. I think about the movie *Fantasia*, the part when the sky is filled with big, dark fluffy clouds, and the old man with the white beard is in the sky on one of them throwing lightning at the people. He goes to bed in it, rolls over, and then goes to sleep, and the cloud goes away to heaven. I think he's God, and I'd like to cover myself with a cloud too, like it's a blanket, but I want a happy one, not an angry one. Throwing the lightning would be fun now that I think about it. I can throw far! When it's sunny, the clouds look like Mom's cotton balls spread out in the sky all around me. She has a ton of them in her bathroom she uses every day to take makeup off. I took one from its box and used it, and Mom saw me and said as I picked bits off my face, "You have to wash your face first. It's not to clean sweat off."

"Why not?"

"Wash your face and stay out of my bathroom." As I took the last bit off, I decided it was stupid to wash my face twice, so I left them alone and just wash my face in the bathtub, but I still sneak in Mom's bathroom sometimes to smell her perfumes and stuff. The clouds look a lot like cotton candy too, except for the pink, and I love it, but not the sticky part.

I look up too, and the clouds aren't fluffy. They're stretched out like white taffy. Auntie's neck is long and pretty, and she stretches it back, and she looks like a statue, the one in my French book, but this statue is naked and she isn't. Her hair is different too. It's short and the lady statue has long hair, some of it in a bun, but she still looks like one anyway because she doesn't move at all. Only her lips do like when you kiss someone, when the smoke comes out, but it takes a long time for that to happen. She sees me, puts her cigarette out right on home plate, then bends down and puts her arms out to me. I skip over.

"I got these for Daddy." She rests her hands on my shoulders. "That's nice; go inside to your mother." Her voice is crackly like she just woke-up, so she clears it. She pretends to smile and it makes me feel weird, and she wants to hug me but stops, and that's weirder because she loves to hug and kiss me more than my other aunts do, and her eyes are watery, but it's not like she's crying, and she shakes a little, but it's not cold. She stands up, takes a cigarette from the pack in her pocket, puts it in her mouth and walks away. She shakes while she lights it.

Uncle is sitting at the kitchen table. I smile and say, "I got these for Daddy." He takes and separates them one at a time and then puts them on the table before he rests a hand on top of them. He takes me into his chest with his other arm. I can hardly breathe, so I wiggle a lot and he lets me go. He looks at my face, but he doesn't see me. I see Daddy in his eyes and the bad butterflies come. He crushes the stems. "My flowers!" He puts them aside and covers his eyes. I take the flowers and run.

At the bottom of the stairs, I hear Mom crying. The last time she cried was when she was pregnant with my brother. She came into the breakfast room carrying lunch with tears on her face. Daddy saw them too, and the bowls didn't break after they smacked the table. She left, picked up her plate and ate at the kitchen sink like always. I forget how to go up the stairs. Maybe it's Mom's crying that makes me forget?

Jesus is at the stairs too. I guess he stayed overnight after he came to my bedroom last night. The wind blew so much the curtains filled up like the sheets on the clothesline and the night bugs were loud and when I rolled over, there he was. His dark, wavy hair looks like mine and our skin is the same color, but his eyes are brown, not blue. He has a nice face like he would never tease or be mean to me, soft and smooth like a china doll, and he smiles at me like we're friends. His white robe has a belt that looks like a rope, like the kind on the clothesline, but it's a little bigger but not as big as rope for a swing. I can't see his feet, just his face and hands which are out to the sides. Light comes out of his fingers, and I can't move, and I have the best butterflies ever! He tells me, "Your father is going to die. I will always take care of you." He gets smaller and smaller, backing up until he is gone. I don't believe anything he says. I pretend his words are leaves that dance with the wind. They move above my head, but they never come down. The butterflies go away, and my legs start fighting with the sheets until they are so tired, I fall asleep.

It's Jesus's words, not my mom's crying, that make me not go upstairs. It's hard to stand up; my knees keep bending. *He's not dead... he's not! He's getting better, the doctors said so.* My head hurts now, but it's not a headache... it's jumbly in there. *They said so! I'm being good, really I am!* A million thoughts bang into me. *I saw you before school… the scar is way better now.* Things are fuzzy like when my nose is stuffy. *I'll be good, I promise!* I can't breathe good either, just like after my brother hit a basketball with a baseball bat right into my stomach on purpose. I grab hold of the railing and go, but I don't climb the stairs myself. *Is that you, Jesus?*

"Go to your mother," Grandma says as our eyes meet at the top of the stairs. Hers are red and swollen like she got stung by a bee there.

"No!" I take my sweater off and cover my eyes and cry.

"Go to your father, comfort your mother." I peek at her and she points down the hall.

The hallway is longer than ever, like a tunnel on *The Road Runner.* The bad butterflies won't stop. *I don't want to! I don't want to!* They keep turning, hard and fast. *It's not real! He's okay! I saw him!* My stomach aches. The flowers are bent, and they fall out of my hand. Everything is blurry… I can't see Grandma anymore. The walls are gone. It's hard to find the bedroom door. *This is a dream, right?* My hand is on the knob and I rub it. *I don't want to!* I turn it. *I don't know what to do!* I tip toe inside.

Daddy's arm moves because Mom is holding his hand and rocking. The sheet covers everything but his feet. His skin looks different. It's kinda see through and I see veins everywhere. It's blue too but not like Robin eggs. His blue is like the color of my old jeans Mom lets me wear on Saturdays.

Her crying is loud, and I cover my ears with the sweater. "I'm a widow! I'm a widow! What am I going to do, what am I going to do!?" I can't see her eyes because her glasses are steamy like the kitchen windows after she makes hot cereal in winter, and she looks likes my sister did when she had the measles. "Say goodbye to your father." *No!* I yell inside because my voice doesn't work right now, and my knees don't either. I fall to the ground and put my sweater over my head.

It's not real! Everything is the same. Please let everything be the same… Daddy please! You're my Brave Girl. I hear his words, but they don't mean the same thing anymore. *I'm not your Brave Girl,* I cry back. I pray with all my might to God behind my sweater. *Please! Let him stay!*

My catechism teacher doesn't teach me about this part, just about the after part: Heaven. That's where angels live with God and everything is perfect. I think it has lots and lots of flowers. It has to because they are the prettiest things around. I like trees too, the ones with flowers more than the other kind. But I can't think about this right now. because lots of stuff goes around in my brain.

Are you still here? Where are you going? Is your angel helping you get there? Is it neat to see him? I want to see mine. When are you coming back? I promise to be good, really good, so don't die anymore, okay? Come back and we can be the same except I'll be better! Are you going to heaven? Just for a visit, right? Can you see God? What does he look like? Can you hear me? Daddy, Daddy? Jesus's words are there too: *I will always take care of you. I don't care what you say, I don't love you anymore!* Monsignor Casey comes in. I run away and my sweater tries to come with me, but I kick it off my foot and leave it on the floor.

Behind the server in the dining room where no one can see me, I sit in a ball with my arms wrapped around my knees. I don't know where Daddy is, and I try to be brave but I can't help it. I keep sobbing. My eyes are on my knees and they keep sliding and they sting too. Parts of my face are dry and there's something on it like sand but it's not that, and there's a salty taste in my mouth, and the sandy stuff is in it too.

It hurts Daddy! Inside me it hurts and won't go away, like someone took something out of me, like they did with you, and now it's empty in there. My stomach aches like the time I rode the merry mixer right after I ate a hot dog real fast. Is God punishing me? Mom says God punishes me when I'm not good and I took Linda's purse. I don't know why I did. I don't even like it, but something inside told me to. I put it back the next day, so does it matter? And Auntie told me God wants you in heaven. Is this right? Why would God take you away when he has so many people already there? Who will take care of me? Is He the boss of everything? I'm waiting for my angel Daddy but I don't feel her. Is she punishing me too?

What's that noise? It sounds like a lot of feet on the floor and I come out from my hiding spot and see two men holding a black bag at the top of the stairs. *Who are you? Get away from him! Get away from him, now! You can't have him!* I run back to the server so fast I trip over myself and fall on my stinging knees, but I don't care anymore.

As I get back to my hiding place, the voices say, "Be careful, to the left, slowly so I can follow. Now back up a little. Get the door." The door closes. *Where are they taking you? Wait! I'm coming too!*

8
Alone

This place is so quiet. The music has no words and it makes me want to take a nap. The people here keep their hands folded in front of them. Maybe they're praying for Daddy? I'm not praying. I'm still mad at God and Jesus. He said he'd take care of me, but how is he going to do that? He's not here, and he's not my daddy.

The room is big with lots of chairs lined up in straight rows. Miss Taylor likes it when we line our chairs up in a straight line too, but these chairs are really straight. I don't want to touch one in case I move it by mistake. It's bad enough I have to be here with all these grown- ups who walk all around me. Talk, talk, talk, that's all they do like this is a party or something. I'm glad I'm in the front row because no one wants to be there. It's close to Daddy, and I don't think they want to look at him. They look over to him, but not at him. They stay away from the front row, that's for sure.

I like the swirls in the carpet. They look like yellow brick roads but they're not yellow, and they look like Dairy Queen ice cream too, but I'm not going to think about ice cream now, but I would like some, dipped in chocolate in a cone. Daddy bought me ice cream at the drive-in. It was so much fun to go there. We'd take the beach wagon and Daddy backed it into the spot and then he'd put the tailgate down and we'd lie in the back and watch *Herbie the Love Bug*. That movie was okay, but I wanted to see a cartoon. I did like when the man and woman kissed in the end.

I want to walk on a swirl and pretend it's the yellow brick road, but I can't because it's a funeral home and walking on a yellow brick road is not allowed. I pretend I am in my head, but this isn't fun, no fun at all, and I want to do something fun instead of running out of tears all the time.

The curtains are smooth, like the ones at the movie theater. They go from the ceiling to the floor, but I don't like the color because it's dark and it makes the room look sad. The lights aren't bright either, and this makes the room sadder.

I rubbed my hand on the curtains when I walked in. They're like Grandmas fancy pillows, the ones I get in trouble for touching. They're so soft I can't help it… I like touching things. Some make me happy, others don't. They hurt sometimes too, like the pointy stuff on the walls at school. Others help me stay awake or fall asleep.

I don't know what to do, and there's nowhere to go. My head itches and so do my stockings. I didn't want to wear them, but I have to because it's a wake and everyone dresses up for it. That's what Mom says. I think wakes are stupid. Everything is sad but no one except me and my brothers and sisters act like it, and no one sees me either, and I wish they did and wanted to be with me and help me feel better. Mom can't be with me because she has to talk to everyone and be kinda okay because that's what grown-ups have to do when it's sad.

My chair is squishy, and I try not to make any noise because Mom says I need to be quiet, but it's hard to be quiet and sit in this chair even if it is squishy. I'm hungry too, but I'm not supposed to be hungry or anything. Well, I am hungry and tired and sick of all of this! I want things to be the same again, like when Daddy was alive. I hate that he's dead. Hate, hate, hate it! Daddy made things all right. Who's going to tell me everything will be all right now? And who's going to tell me what to do besides be quiet, quiet, quiet, like a good little girl whose daddy is dead. I just want to run away and hide.

So many people are here to see Daddy. All the seats are taken, and people are standing in the back by the curtains. I turn around and look for a second. Some are crying now and that makes me happy. Isn't that weird? But it's true because now I know they love him like I do and they get it, and this makes me feel a little better. The talkers keep talking and they're making me angry. They don't care about Daddy, so why are they here? And the ones I see smiling make me mad and I want them to leave right now! They don't love Daddy like I do. They can't and smile at the same time. Daddy is gone and it's terrible without him so stop talking and smiling! The other people just sit and wait, but I don't know what they are waiting for. Daddy's casket is all there is.

It's in the front of the room with lights shining on it from the ceiling. They're the only bright ones in the room. It looks like Daddy is on a stage and we're the audience. Does he know everyone is watching him? He looks like he's in a wooden bed and asleep, but I know he's not and besides, he couldn't sleep with those bright lights shining on him anyway. The wood is dark and shiny, and it looks smooth and I want to touch it and it has handles on the sides with shiny metal rings around them. They twinkle in the light like blinkers on a Christmas tree. Half of it is open where Daddy's head and body are. The other half is closed. Daddy is still on his back, lying on a shiny white sheet that isn't smooth like the sheet on my bed. It puckers. This is what grandma says, and she knows because she sews. It puckers all around him, even inside the open top part there is a sheet that puckers. He looks like the star out there on the stage. He is the most important person in the room even though he's dead.

There are lots of flowers all around the casket in different holders and a lot of colors, mostly red. On top of it are red roses. They don't look like the ones Mom grows in her garden. These are dark red with long stems. There are too many to count, and they cover everything but the open part of it. There are flowers I don't know, sorta roundish, sorta like the pom-poms in art class, and they're not as pretty as roses. Some flowers are the same as those Mom puts outside when it's Halloween. I think she calls them mums.

I keep my hand hidden on my side and rub the wood. My hand slides back and forth so easy and my knees stop bending so much. Daddy's face isn't blue anymore. It's my color and his cheeks are pink, and his lips are red, almost like Mom's lipstick. He is dressed like when he and Mom go out to a party: white shirt with folds on the front, black buttons, and a bow around his neck. I can't see his pants because the sheet covers him there. His hair is combed back like it always is. He's holding a cross with Jesus on it.

I can tell no one around me sees what I'm doing either, but do they see what I see? I don't think they do because some keep staring, and the talkers keep talking. It's very warm by Daddy and I see the air whirling around me. I see goldish color in it and it looks like the stuff Tinker Bell has… you know, pixie dust. It's sorta foggy like when I walk to school in the morning just when spring starts and it's wet like outside in August. I want to sit down but there isn't a chair and I'm not supposed to touch the casket, but I do because my knees are bending again. I look back at Mom to make sure I'm not in trouble but she's not looking at me. She's busy with people who keep going up to her to say, "I'm sorry." What are they sorry about? What did they do? I think they should say, "What happened for God to make John die?" Being sorry doesn't help figure out what went wrong.

Daddy's here to visit. I see the golden color circle around me. It swirls like water in a toilet. *You're my brave girl.* Last time Daddy was alive he said this to me. It was in the morning before school. "Come give me a kiss," he said. It's weird because he sounded far away but he wasn't. "You're my brave girl," he said. "I am!"

"I'm glad you came back… please don't go." I keep looking and looking at him, but he doesn't say anything with his mouth, only in my head. *You're my brave girl… you're my brave girl.* And I say, *I don't want to be your brave girl… I want you here now! And I want this to go away… I want us to stay the same.* I hear nothing. *I can't be brave like this. It's too hard and I don't want to be anyway. It's stupid if it means you're not coming back. I'm not your brave girl—I'm not! I just want to be your girl.*

Some Thing whispers in my head, "*How will you live without Daddy?*" "*I don't know,*" I answer. And then this Thing grabs me. I'm weaker than I ever was and there's nothing left but what used to be me because everything changes. I'm not a little girl anymore. I'm not a grown up either. I'm stuck in the middle of nowhere and it's cold and I have no friends and I have this feeling like everyone is bossing me around and I can't move or think right. But Daddy is here now and it's okay. Everything is going to be okay once he wakes up. Right? Looking across the room, I try to find someone who knows what I know, but no one does. "He's alive," I hear myself say. Some look at me, but they don't listen. I hate all of them. They don't see the real me.

My aunt leans over and says, "It's God's will." Why is this the answer to every important question? All my aunts and my mother say the same thing. "Do what you are supposed to do, and everything will be all right with God." This is another answer I get when I need help. I'm trying to be a good girl. I thought I was doing what I'm supposed to. I took the purse, but I gave it back. I sit on the squishy chair swinging my legs back and forth and I remember tripping on the wooden stairs when I ran up them. I was in trouble. Mom hears my knee bang and I cry out. "God is punishing you," she says. I don't think God likes me very much and whatever I did was really, really bad because Daddy is dead.

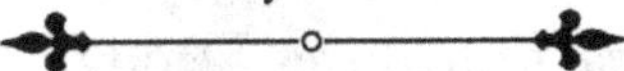

I have my favorite dress on for the funeral. I feel pretty in it and it's not tight and girly so I can run and jump in it if I want to. Daddy bought it for me at his friend's clothes factory. I think he's happy I'm wearing it. "It matches your blue eyes," Mom said when she took it off the rack. What a fun place this was. Clothes everywhere in bright happy colors: greens, oranges, reds, blues and yellows. I got fishnet stockings too, and I have a pair on to match my dress. The factory didn't have shoes, so Mom took me to Stride Rite for them. I picked out patent leather ones, the same ones I scraped on the way home from school, but it's okay. Mom didn't see them, and I polished them as best I could for the funeral.

The long black car takes us to church and the neighbors watch me and my family get in, but no one says "Hello." It's an okay car, the seat is better than the one at the funeral home and it smells good, but the windows are dark and the ride isn't as good as I thought it would be. It's slow and the air is heavy like after you get out of a hot shower and I face everyone but don't talk because there are no words when it's too sad to talk.

The casket is closed, and it's covered with our flag. I think it looks good and is right for Daddy because he was in the war. My brother thinks his uniform is his, but I put it on anyway when he's not looking, and I make sure I close the cellar door too. That's where it's kept. "I told you to leave it alone!" He yells from the top of the stairs. "I can wear it," but I take it off and put it back so he doesn't hit me. It's really big on me. It's green and smells like the army, that's what Mom says, but I don't care because it's Daddy's and he's strong and brave. The round gold pins on the collar say "U.S.," and on the sleeves are two stripes that look like the points of arrows. When I can get away with it, I put it on, button it up, take hold of one of the poles in the middle of the cellar, lean away from it, then drop my head back and spin around it trying not to move my feet, but they get crossed and I almost fall down. I try a couple of more times but then it's hot, so I take it off, kiss it and put it away. Daddy has a baseball jacket from high school, and I want to wear it but my brother gets it because he's older and the boy. It's okay because he loves Daddy like I do and when he's not looking, I put it on sometimes and I feel him and I hope my brother does too. His army blanket is in the cellar with the army jacket and my brother says I can play with that. It's mostly used to make the fort in the family room. I put it over the coffee table and it's dark underneath like a cave and me and my sister play in it and my brother does too when he's not being a jerk.

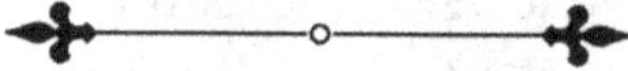

From the car window I watch my cousins and uncles lift Daddy's casket up the church stairs. Their faces are crinkled up and it takes a long time to get him to the doors. It's sprinkling raining when I get out of the long car. A man in black opens an umbrella above my head. I'm special today and I like it, but the bad butterflies come. When you're special you should have good ones.

At the top of the stairs, lots of people are standing around the doors of the church. They are wearing black and gray. Gramma tells me that these are the colors to wear.

"But I'm in blue," I say.

"You're a child. It's different for you." Seems like everything is different for kids when their Daddy dies. It's hard but I look through and around them and see the benches are filled up. There are even people against the walls. Wow! I knew Daddy was an important man, but I didn't know he had so many friends. It's mostly quiet but some people whisper, and it looks like everyone is very nice and there is lots of hugging and patting on the back. Some help other people get to a pew. But some people are smiling again. I don't get them. My catechism teacher is on my right against the wall by herself. She holds a handkerchief to her eyes.

The first prayer she taught me was the *Our Father*. She had me fold my hands at my desk, sit up straight, and recite it with the other kids. I'm fine until I say, "Thy will be done on earth as it is in heaven." I keep saying it, but the other kids stop after the word 'done'. There isn't a comma in the sentence and that's why I don't stop like Mrs. Taylor taught me and I know I'm right because I'm in the highest reading group, but my teacher says I should anyway, so I do.

"God made the world," my teacher says. I learn what man is but not woman. I guess we're the same except for the private parts but I really want to know for sure. Did you know God made me to know, love, and serve Him here? The Church teaches me how to do all this and if I do it right, I get to go to Heaven. Daddy doesn't go to church. He reads the paper while we're there, and when I get home, I read the comics. Can Daddy know and love God without going to church?

I'm still waiting to go into the church, and I can't see anything in front of me except a piece of the flag on top of the casket and so many more people are coming in that the doors stay open and there's no place for them and it's raining harder so it's getting wet inside too. My hands are very sticky, and I wipe them on my dress. My forehead is wet, and I bend down fast and wipe it with my dress and then I try to unstick my hair from my face and unglue my stockings from my legs.

It's hard to breathe and the people who see me shake their heads from side to side and stare with sad faces. *Don't look at me! I see! I see him!* They move all around me, clearing a way for me and my family to go into the church. I fix myself as best I can, taking the hair off my face and pulling the stockings from my legs again. There isn't any room for me to bend down and dry the patent leather on my shoes. The priest comes in through the doors and so do others dressed in white robes. Everyone gets out of their way as they move through them until I can't see them anymore.

I have to go in and see all those people I don't know now, and I don't know what to do or how to be brave like Daddy wants. *What if I mess it up? Where are you, guardian angel?* Daddy is in my head with me. *You're my brave girl… you're my brave girl.* I look ahead and see more of the flag. It's moving down the aisle and I do too. I bite my lip when the music plays. *I'm your brave girl?* I see the casket in front of me as I step onto the red carpet. Everyone is standing, everyone's eyes are following the casket as it's carried down the aisle. Everything is very, very quiet and very, very serious, and then I know what to do. *I am your brave girl, Daddy.* I follow him for the last time, standing tall, with my head up and my arms by my side to the front row where I sit with my family.

9

Sweet Sorrow

One of the dumb boys in my class brings a story about Daddy in for show and tell, and the bad butterflies come back. It's been two weeks since the funeral and I'm trying really hard to forget he's dead. The stupid boy shows it to the class, and I sink in my seat. I want to crawl under my desk but I'm too scared to do that. I hope no one is looking at me.

I can see Daddy's picture and I remember seeing it at home on a book or something in a box Mom put in the attic. She told me he wanted to be elected to something, but I can't remember what it was and the book had information about him for people to read and see if they wanted to pick him. He did this a long time ago because the picture is old. It doesn't look like my daddy. It looks like my daddy before he was my daddy.

This boy isn't the best reader, so he won't know all the words in the story, but I do because I read it in the newspaper that comes to the house. Now the tears are coming, and the butterflies don't stop. When he starts to read it out loud, Miss Taylor stops him.

"Okay, that's enough. Does anyone have something else to share?"

My classmates ask me questions about Daddy and want to know everything about cancer and stuff like that and what it's like to have a dead father and I'm holding back my tears trying to be brave but it's hard and I just want to scream and run away.

Miss Taylor finds me in the corner facing the wall and my brain is thinking a lot and it hurts bad.

Everyone knows. I'm different now. I'm the girl without a daddy and everyone has a daddy, everyone! I can't talk about it. I won't. I hate this! Where can I go? I want to hide and not come out, not ever! You can't be dead, not really… you can't! Why did you leave me? Where did you go? I thought maybe you are in Heaven, Daddy, but is there a secret? Are you someplace else and can't tell me? Please let this be it. Please, please, please!

Miss Taylor hands me a tissue. "Here, do you want to go to the counselor's office?"

I go just to get away from everyone and I don't even touch the wall as I walk to his office because I'm afraid I'll get pricked again.

He says, "How are you today?"

"I don't know." I pick up the doll on the table.

"What are you doing in class?"

"Reading and stuff." I sit down.

"Are you getting your work done?"

"Sometimes, but I don't want to work. I'm tired."

"Miss Taylor says you're with the nurse during recess."

I nod.

"Don't you want to play with your friends?"

"I don't feel like it."

"I thought you loved recess."

"That was before."

"And now?"

"I don't feel like it. I'm tired."

"I see you looking at that book. Do you want to read it?"

"What's it about?"

"Feelings. Maybe what you feel is here, in this book."

"I don't think I feel anything."

I think Daddy is alive and on a secret mission. He goes far away, and the people are very poor, and they hurt and need help and Daddy helps them because that's what he does. They don't have to pay him like the people he helped here, and they love him like I do. But I miss him, and I wish he would call me and let me know he is okay. I want to tell Mom, but I don't think she'll believe me. She thinks Daddy is dead for good, so we don't go to the cemetery anymore because she says it's better not to and that's okay because I hate it there.

There is a sign on the ground that has Daddy's name on it and his birthday and death day, and I do the math in my head. He is forty-four years old forever. There is a round thing next to the sign that tells people he was in the war. This place is scary, but I think the round thing is neat. I'm just standing here looking all around and see nothing but green grass, fake flowers, and some flags. Mom says Daddy's with the Catholics. The Jewish people are across the street. It's too quiet and I have to make sure I don't walk on the graves because it's wrong and I'm in enough trouble with God already and I think there must be other girls like me who made Him very angry too because there are a lot of dead people here. I'm glad we're not going back. It's sad and scary and I don't like to think of Daddy there by himself in the ground where its cold. He doesn't have a blanket.

In the nighttime, I lie in bed with the curtains open and stare at the sky. I think about Daddy helping people and I think about me and him too.

"Do rumpzeedumepst... do it, Daddy." I blow the hair away from my eyes.

"Are you ready?"

"Yes!"

"Hold on."

I wrap my arms around his legs and hold on tight. He says, "A rumpzeedumepst... a rumpzeedumepst..."

His made-up word is funny, and I hold on when he walks across the yard, stretching my arms until they are straight, and I tilt my head so far back my short hair drags along on the ground. I mouth the word in my head, *rumpzeedumepst... rumpzeedumepst.*

He stops at the breezeway. "All done with rumpzeedumepst."

"Don't stop Daddy. Please do it again!"

No more rumpzeedumepst… no more rumpzeedumepst. That Thing is back, and it tells me I will forget everything about Daddy soon. It says Time will take him and I'll have nothing left except some pictures from long ago like the picture of us from my first communion. I'm sad and mad at the same time, so I keep thinking because if I think about it for a long time I won't forget.

The house is old and white with a big front porch, squeaking floors, big windows and an old piano. The only songs I can play are Chopsticks and Heart and Soul. Daddy rented it last summer. I love this old house and I run through it with my sandy feet and water drips on the floor and I don't get yelled at because it's an old house and Mom doesn't care. I even drag my towel around and she doesn't get mad when sand gets on the floor! Me and my sister play jacks on it and eat lunch there too. My brother builds a bunch of models at the kitchen table and he doesn't get in trouble when he gets glue on it! This is the best house in the world, and I want to live here forever!

The yard doesn't have grass and who cares? I run around it anyway and it's filled with flowers Mom calls weeds, but they are pretty, too. The white ones are the best. They have a big flat flower and on top that looks like a lot of little flowers connected and it doesn't have leaves. It has like seaweed leaves. There are dandelions too, and I pick them for Gramma and she makes soup with them for Grandpa. Yuck!

I can see the ocean from my house, and if I try real hard, I can throw a rock from the end of the driveway to the beach as long as I run first. It's so wicked to see it make it. I go there every day and walk, swim and collect seashells. My favorite thing is lying on the sand and staring at the sky and dreaming. I can't remember what I dream about, but it's fun. The seagulls try to take my food and I let them if it's sandy. I mean, I ate a bologna sandwich that fell in the sand and it was okay, so sometimes I eat stuff when it's sandy if I'm real hungry. I don't go home until the sun is just on top of the water, and I wish I was old enough to stay at the beach at night. I bet it's pissah. All I can do is leave my window open to listen to the ocean sing and watch the moon shine on it. I think they're friends and I think they play when people are sleeping.

Me and my brother go to the penny candy store a lot. He plays his radio, and there's always the same song. I know the words and sing it when I walk. "Come on baby light my fire, come on baby light my fire… try to set the night on fire." I can't help it, my hips swing and my arms wave as we go. Daddy and Mom go to see Rosemary's Baby at the movies. I hear them say it is scary, so I don't want to see it and I go to the gas station with Daddy because it's giving away free Red Sox cards when you get gas. I want Carl Yastrzemski but end up with Tony Conigliaro and Daddy says, "He's good and Italian like us." So, now I'm glad I have Tony, but I still want Carl too.

"Are you watching?" I yell from the bottom of the beach. Daddy waves from the top of it. He just got here from work in the city and still has his shoes on. He's so funny! I see his white teeth and he has his hands on his hips. I let my kite go and I run down the beach in front of him. Its tail wags like Cinders', the dog next door at home.

"Do you see it, Daddy?"

He waves and nods.

"Watch how high I can make it go!" I let the string out too fast and the kite moves all over the place before it gets straight again and flies right. I lean to the right and it goes there and then I lean to the left, back and forth and I go side to side with it and I look at Daddy who smiles at me and then goes to the house.

We stand at the kitchen counter and I watch him undo prosciutto from the wrapper. "Hurry up Daddy!" My hands flap and I jump up and down as he picks up the meat. He's so good and he never tears it. I'm always in a hurry so I always tear it and he laughs at me and shows me how to do it right. My mouth waters when I crumple a piece and pop it in my mouth. It melts there and then slides down my throat.

"More, more!"

"Just a minute, my turn now."

I remember football games in our backyard with the boys. Daddy coaches us from the big tree and he throws for both sides. "I'm ready Daddy! Throw it to me!" I push dummy Duncan McQueen down and he rolls on the ground. "Throw it!" He throws and I catch it and run to the patio. "Touchdown!" Daddy's hands are on his hips.

"Girls can do anything boys do!"

"Let's go!" Daddy's yelling but smiling too.

Remember rumpzedumst, Daddy? I stand on your feet and hold on to your legs and we walk around the yard? You say rumpzedumst and I don't know what it means, but I don't care because it's funny. How about the beach house? I fly my kite for you, and I make you smile. It goes so high and it looks like a ballerina in the sky. And you take me to the gas station every week so I can collect Red Sox baseball cards. I miss our trips to the drive-in in the beach wagon and the times you took me to Boston to buy meats and the drug store too. You always let me get a candy bar or baseball cards while you buy cigars and even though they smell gross and I hate when you smoke them in the car. I promise never to feel like this again if you come back. Mom hasn't bought prosciutto since you left, and I miss it like everything else.

I'm starting to forget things like how to separate prosciutto from the paper like you taught me, your voice, the way you laugh and how you write your name. I look at your pictures and sometimes they tell me things about you, like this is me when I was a boy. Look how tall and skinny I am! This is me when I'm in the army. I'm strong and do the best I can to help our side win. There are some pictures that look like you but they make me sad so I only look at the old ones. Every time I think about you, I cry. I want you to talk to me, but I don't hear you right now. Did you forget me? Please say no. I can't take it if you don't want me around anymore. I miss you so much I can't breathe sometimes.

Something warm is in my room. I don't move under the covers and I'm not sure what to do, but I open my eyes and stare out the window. The stars twinkle like a million fireflies. I know the Big Dipper and the Little Dipper but nothing else and I play connect the dots with the stars and make shapes, but I like doodling better. Is Heaven somewhere up there where I can see it? I hope it's warm and colorful with lots of flowers.

I can't see the sky right now because there is a bubble around me that makes everything outside look cloudy. What is that tingling feeling in my body? It's not the good or bad butterflies. It's a new feeling, like goose bumps, but my skin stays the same and the tingling doesn't go away. I feel different, lighter, and the bed is lighter too and it doesn't feel like my bed. It's almost like I'm on a fluffy cloud just as I imagined lying on my back by the oak tree. I don't move until I feel something on the mattress. I turn over. It's Daddy! I stare and my tears come out of my eyes and go down my face. He's in his work clothes and I know the white shirt, black pants and dark red tie. He doesn't have his ring or watch on because they're in a box in Mom's room. Everything else is the same. His hair, eyes, smile and the way he sits. His arms stretch out, reaching for me, and I sit up and reach back and the tingling feeling turns around and around like the twister in *The Wizard of Oz.*

10
New Life

Daddy's been gone for almost three years. His stuff is in the cellar, a picture of an old Harvard against Yale football game and a painted poster of him made when he was picked All American tight end of New England. His uniform from the war is still there too. All his pictures and stuff and knives from the war are in the attic in a box that says "John." My brother likes the knives, and he picks them up and looks real close at them. "This came from an infantryman and this was an officer's. I wonder how he got it?"

"Who cares?"

"You don't get it."

I don't. They're heavy and sharp and I know what they do. My brother tells me Daddy took them from dead soldiers, and I don't like to think about that. I ask, "Did he do good stuff?"

"He helped liberate a concentration camp."

"I bet that was gross."

"Maybe that's where he got this." He holds up the officer's knife to the light. "Dirty Kraut!"

The pictures of Daddy from the war show him smiling and clean. He doesn't look anything like the boys from the war we watched on TV.

"He fought before he became an MP. He saw and did things," my brother says.

"Nothing bad!"

"Nothing is good in war, don't you get it?"

I still don't and sometimes I go in the attic alone and look at Daddy's stuff by myself. I put the knives in one pile and all the other stuff like pictures and the playbills with notes on them in another. One says, "the play was good, but the acting stunk." Daddy drew squiggly lines around the work "stunk" and it looks like the word smells. Those other things I decide belong to him and the knives are just there, kinda like anything that is old and packed away for no good reason.

Daddy and Mom's wedding picture is in a drawer downstairs in the dining room. His clothes have been gone for a long time from his dresser and closet and Mom uses it for storage, and his dresser is empty except for these cards: Sons of Italy, Rotary Club, Elks Club, Knights of Columbus. They have his name on them and he had them in his wallet with some handkerchiefs he carried in his pants pocket. They smell like Old Spice.

I shuffle the cards and lay them in a very straight line and talk to him in my head. *You are very important, Daddy. I remember all the people who came to the church. You were a good man, and everyone liked you. They told me so after the funeral and I was proud, and I still think about you all the time. I can say your name without crying now, but not for too long. I still pretend you're on a secret mission, but I know the truth. Pretending is a habit, that's all.* I kiss each card like I'm kissing him, and I miss him all over again. Mom says Daddy liked being away. That's why he was in so many clubs. I don't believe her. I close the dresser and try to be very quiet because I don't want her to hear me. She's in her bathroom getting ready, and she wants me to forget about Daddy like she has.

This is what happens on Sundays now. I don't go to church anymore because it's "too much." That's what Mom says, and it's okay because I'm still mad at God and Jesus isn't my friend anymore either. I miss the music, but I still sing at religion school at Christmas time. I wait for her to come out.

Sitting on the bedroom chair with a heart shaped back, I run my hand one way until it is the same shade of blue and then, I run it the other until it is the other, lighter blue. I keep doing this because I'm hungry. I count the buttons on the back. One, two, three, four across the top… one, two, three, four, five across the middle… one, two, three, four across the bottom. Thirteen… *When are you coming out? You said we could have bacon and eggs and maybe go to the mall.* I'm not sure we'll go shopping. Mom says she'll take me but then doesn't because it gets too late, but she stays in the bathroom the whole time! That's why we can't go! I don't remember her doing it before Daddy died, but she does all the time now. "It's the only place I can go to get away from you brats," she says. I don't say anything back. What can I say? I count more buttons, the ones I sit on. One, two, three at the back… one, two, three, four in the second row… one, two, three, four, five in the middle and… one, two, three, four on the front. Sixteen.

Mom doesn't like our new life either. She tells me, "Your father died and left me with all you kids." I'm trying to behave, but I'm not good at it. I sit around a lot and "mope." Mom taught me the word, and it's a good one for me right now.

She says that I don't feel good about myself and I let things get to me and act not normal about them and that I can't make a good decision. "You're insecure, but that's because of your father's death," she says. "His death created problems for all of us." I don't see how Daddy dying gave us problems. He's the one who got it bad because he's dead, and I don't like not being able to decide things, and I think I can, but I don't try. I want to make my own decisions. I really do! It's like I can't talk or something and that Thing is always with me somehow and It holds me back. Sometimes it's real close and sometimes I don't feel it for a week or two. That's when I'm the happiest and I know I can think for myself, but right now Mom makes most decisions for me and I let her because she's my mom and she knows best. I can tell my feelings aren't right by Mom's voice. It's like I'm sick or something. The thing is, she doesn't tell me how to fix it. She just says that I am… you know… these things and there's no medicine for it. Well, she hasn't given me any yet. I feel like I'm always being looked at up close, like I'm a fish in a tank. It's weird, and I can't make a move without thinking I'm wrong. All I know is I don't think I'm good enough anymore. I don't remember feeling like this when Daddy was alive.

"When I was your age, I was running errands in Boston for my mother," Mom says. "She trusted me, not my sisters." I listen to her, and I know this is the beginning of one of those times she needs to talk about her life when she was my age. The story is always the same.

"My mother trusted me to get food, so I went with war stamps, but sometimes I was scared, and men looked at me and came close. My sisters never had to go. They never did anything; one was in her own world drawing or painting and the other couldn't be trusted, always getting into trouble, and I had to bail her out, fighting for her, even taking her SATs because my mother didn't think she could do well on them. The scores got her into BU, but I was so scared I'd get caught and then kicked out of Vassar. I had to beg my parents to let me go there. They didn't understand what I wanted to do, but they let me go, and I had to go interview before they'd let me into the college." Mom pauses.

"My name... do you think there were many Italians there? There weren't, and they wanted to make sure I was a fit. It took a long time for your grandfather to break into Pinebrook Country Club, but he did. My friends became lawyers and doctors later on, after they married." Mom looks ahead at nothing. "I came home and got married and did nothing else. I wanted to, but my parents wanted me to marry. That's what was expected of me. My parents didn't know any better coming from their backgrounds, and neither did I. They're old world that way. I didn't have a role model to follow, not like you have with me. It'll be better for you because you're second generation. First generation has to figure it all out."

She sighs. "It was awful living in Everett after we got married. We had no privacy, and your father could be mean, and he tried to hit me. My God, you should have heard his parents fight! No wonder your father acted as he did. I wanted to get out of there, and when I told my mother, she sent me back. 'You made your bed.' These were her words."

I don't like when Mom tells me this kind of stuff. The bad butterflies come, but she keeps going. "You think your father was so great? Well, let me tell you, he wasn't. He didn't like women and he smelled, but he called it, 'Man's odor.' God! He wanted me to work with him, but I wasn't going to work myself into the ground and make it easier for the next wife. No way! I thought about divorcing him." *Please stop!* My head pounds, but I just sit and listen and don't say a word. Last time I did, it was bad.

"You don't know what you're talking about so be quiet!" she said.

"But…"

"Shut up!"

And my being a tomboy doesn't help. "You're the wreck of the Hesperus." She says this a lot when I come in from playing. I think Hesperus is a little girl from a long time ago who climbs trees, swims in a reservoir, and does what boys do. She also says, "Why are you doing the Saint Vitus dance?" I think this might be a good thing because it has the word saint in it, but I'm not sure, and I learn not to ask questions about these things because they aren't answered. My knees are a mess, dirty and scraped. Why is it okay for boys to get dirty but not girls? I like to get dirty, so I think there is a mistake and I should have been born a boy. Daddy didn't care when I was dirty. He liked it when I was like a boy. I sit facing the back of the chair and place all five fingers on the buttons at once and then move them to another five buttons.

"Are you almost finished?" I ask with my mouth pressed against the door. I turn my head and place my right ear on the door and wait.

Silence.

"Mom?"

Silence.

"When are you coming out? I'm hungry. I've been waiting for a long time."

Silence.

Sitting on the floor stretching my legs underneath the chair, I try to stick all ten fingers in ten different buttonholes. I scratch the buttons but not well because I bite my nails.

I say it louder, "Mom, are you done?"

Silence.

"Are you through?"

"Leave me alone!"

I go into Mom's dresser, crinkling the tissue no matter how carefully I try to unwrap what's inside. I turn my head several times toward the bathroom door to make sure she doesn't hear the noise and figure out what I'm doing. I look in the mirror and smooth down my messy hair with the palms of my hands before I take one of the pieces from the tissue paper and place it on my head. It's fake hair in a bun. I'm not so good at doing hair, so it's hard to put it on with the couple of bobby pins next to it, and then it looks stupid, so I take it off and get the other piece. Mom calls this a fall. It's fake hair too, and I've only seen her wear it once before Daddy died. She doesn't go out anymore because of me and my brothers and sisters.

"I can't do anything because I have five anchors!" She says, when she is mad and sad at the same time. I don't know who she's mad at, but I know she's not sad about Daddy.

"He'd rather be with his cronies than with us," she tells me. I looked up 'cronies' in the dictionary and it means friends, but Mom made it sound like a bad word. The fall is like half a head of hair, and when I wear it, it looks like I have more hair than I have. It's easier to put on because it rests on top of my head. I turn my head side to side, the hair swishes and I think, *When I grow up, I'll try to be more like a girl is supposed to be.*

After I put the fake hair back and shut the drawer, I walk to the bathroom door and press my left ear to it. I hear sniffles. "When am I going to have a life? Dear God, when am I going to have a life?" She sighs so loud I hear it. *When is she going to have a life, God? You messed it all up, taking Daddy away! Now Mom can't be happy and have a life because she has to stay home and take care of me and everyone else!* I hear her slippers on the floor, louder and louder, and I back up thinking she's going to open the door, but she doesn't. She locks it instead and turns on the shower.

I'm back on the chair still waiting and I'm real hungry now and I feel like jumping and yelling so Mom gets it, but I don't. I swing my legs back and forth. I'm still bored. *Why are you in there so long? What is wrong? Come out!* My legs go crazy and swing by themselves. *I wish Daddy was here. I wish you weren't sad and mad all the time!*

The bathroom door opens, and Mom comes out in a towel. Her hair is in one too, and she goes to her dresser to get her clothes.

"I'm hungry, Mom."

"I'll be down soon, after I get dressed."

"You've been in the bathroom since nine o'clock."

"This is my time. I get dressed once a day and then I'm done." She goes back to the bathroom, shuts the door, and locks it. I'm on the chair again. I wait. It's almost eleven o'clock when she opens the bathroom door, picks up her laundry, turns off the light and goes downstairs. I follow her.

The first time I come home from school and Mom isn't there is hard. I like when she's home. It means everything is the same, all right, but with her not home, I know life is never going to be the same. I sit at the top of the stairs, and I see the men again, those that took Daddy away in the black bag and I think, *Why me? Why do I have to not have a father? And now, Mom is gone too, and I don't want to grow up, but I have to because Mom says she needs help, and I want to help, but I don't want to.* I want to cry, but there aren't any tears, just a burning inside, so I stomp my feet on the stairs over and over instead until it doesn't make sense to do it anymore.

Mom hires a few babysitters first, but they don't work out. "You kids are wild," one says as she leaves in a hurry. Another gets locked in the bathroom after she breaks the doorknob. It has broken before, and I know how to make it work if it gets stuck, but I don't tell her because she's mean and can't cook. She opens the window and screams to the neighbors, "I'm trapped! Help me! Help me!" Me and my brother laugh real hard and then he lets her out. There is one I like, but she doesn't stay long, and I don't know why, and she really likes my younger sister and makes her a sock monkey.

Mom tells us, "I can't keep doing this. You can take care of yourselves from now on, and you can kill each other for all I care."

I take in the mail and sort it into three piles on the counter: bills, checks, and everything else. There is more mail at the beginning of the month, and I make sure I get it all out of the box and don't drop it on the way in. There are a lot of bills: gas, electric, credit cards, mortgage, medical, on and on, and I hate them because they make life harder than it is. Mom comes home from school, opens them up and just keeps looking at them before she puts them in the bill box. The top broke off a while ago but Mom still uses it and it's black, which is a good color for a bill box, I think. I stay way out of the way when it's time to pay bills, but I can see Mom from the family room and sometimes she cries as she writes checks, mostly in the winter when she pays the gas bill. I know it's bad because she turns the heat down. But Mom always cooks, and our house and clothes are always clean.

She leaves food on the stove for me to finish cooking before she goes out. She attends classes at night, studies, and takes care of us during the day. She is tired a lot, and she doesn't have time for stories and prayers like other moms, but I'm learning it's okay. She works hard and many nights she falls asleep at the dining room table while she's doing homework. Cooking is not so bad, and I'm getting better at it. Like I said, I don't want to grow up right now. I want to come home from school and do nothing, eat snacks, and play. If my brother isn't there, I can watch what I want on TV, game shows and cartoons, but growing up makes me feel good sometimes, like when I take care of my baby brother. He's so cute and he loves me just the way I am. Cooking for him is worth it. Tonight, I'm making beef over rice. Mom already cut up the meat and cooked it part way. All I have to do is finish cooking it and the rice. I don't like measuring, like I have to do with the rice. It takes too much time, and I want to get supper over with before my brother starts in.

"You know," he says, grinning. "Since you are a going to be a woman, that means you serve men."

"Shut up!"

"Do you know what woman means?"

"You're an ass!"

"Wo means under and you know what man means, so woman means under man. Get it? You're under man, which means you're under me and must serve me."

"I hate you!"

"Like I said, you're going to marry someone just like me." He laughs.

My brother is the smartest person I know. He reads all the time, even when he watches TV. All he cares about is the military, any stories, magazines, or movies about it. I see him reading a book called *Jane's Fighting Ships*. It's filled with pictures of all the ships in the Navy and all the information about them. Talk about boring, but he loves it and keeps reading. He reads real books too, gifts from Daddy's mother, but she doesn't buy me books ever. She teaches me how to paint and bake, but she doesn't want to see me anymore now that Daddy is dead. I feel like I'm dead, too.

Daddy's brother and sister feel the same way, and I miss them and wish they'd come to visit me. One time, Uncle called the house, and I thought it was Daddy. I remembered his voice when I heard Uncle's, and I don't say anything, and it's weird when he keeps talking, and I don't remember what he says, but the bad butterflies come back for a little bit, and after I hang up the phone, I go in the attic to look at pictures to try to feel better.

My brother builds models, so many that he fills his room with them, all navy ships, and he is so fast, he puts them together in a day. I tried to build one, but it was bad and had glue marks all over it. I'm better at sports. He is mad a lot, like Mom, and sad too, because Daddy died, and he gets to go and talk to someone, but it doesn't work because he still calls me "dog" like it's my name and tells me, "You're a girl, that's all." He likes my little sister better, and she's a girl, so I don't get it. Maybe she's the right kind of girl.

After supper, it's time to clean up and my older sister helps me. She's in special classes at school. Mom says, "She has minimal brain dysfunction." All I know is she has problems learning, but she teaches me to read a clock, my times table and how to count money. I don't understand her though, why she acts weird sometimes and runs away from the house when she's upset. I hope no one sees her. We're not friends, and sometimes we talk, but it's hard because all she wants to talk about is her music. Tom Jones is one of her favorites, and I hear her singing from her bedroom, "What's new pussycat, whoa whoa whoa whoa whoa…" She also talks about her weight. "One hundred and sixteen!" she yells from the bathroom after she weighs herself. She listens to the radio mostly, rocking in her chair or banging her head on her pillow.

She has a hard time when Daddy is sick, and on the nights he coughs a lot, she screams from her bed, "Shut up Daddy. *Shut up!*" And when he keeps doing it, she keeps going, louder and louder until he gets so upset, he comes out of his room and tells her to stop. She says, "I won't stop! Shut up!" After the funeral, she says, "Daddy is dead... Daddy is dead."

"Shut up," I say.

"God did it, you know. He did it." From then on, the radio, her weight *and* God are all she talks about. "God makes your hair grow... God makes your weight... God did it... He did." She gets angry, throws things or swears, and then says, "God made me do it. He made me, you know." One night, she is standing over my head as I lie in bed.

"What are you doing?"

"I'm going to smother you."

"No, you're not. Go back to bed, okay?"

"Okay, I'm sorry. God made me do it."

"I know."

She scrubs the pot and pan and rinses the sink and I load the dishwasher. Mr. Berry just fixed it the other night. He is our handyman and I call him Uncle Berry after a while. Sometimes, I sit with him when he's working on the washer or the oven or the plumbing, and I learn about tools, and it's nice to have an almost-Daddy around just so I don't forget what it's like. My baby brother likes him a lot too and spends more time with him than I do. He's very nice to Mom and doesn't make her pay a lot of money for stuff. He's like Daddy that way. I wipe down the counters and sink and then sweep. I turn off all the lights except the one above the sink, make sure the kitchen door is locked and give my baby brother a bath. My sister goes upstairs to her room and rocks while she listens to WRKO.

11

The bus ride from Arlington Heights to downtown Lexington is not scenic. It's a straight shot down Massachusetts Avenue, a sixteen-mile thoroughfare of blacktop that runs through Boston's industry, historic neighborhoods and thriving suburbs. Strip malls fill in the mundane spaces. I ride just long enough for the word to sink in. Pregnant, pregnant. There should be joy, there should be warmth, hope and expectation, but there is nothing except loneliness. It does not matter who the father is or the fact he wants this to go away.

"Don't go home," he says.

"I have to go."

"Come back here. This is our responsibility. We'll take care of this quietly."

"I'll call you later." The words I had hoped to hear are not spoken and I cannot offer them myself. I hang up the phone, buy a bus ticket and get on board without thought or feeling. My destination is too much to bear, but I am unable to choose another path.

I understand the Thing. His name is Fear, and he is my constant companion and the reason I struggle. I have moments of clarity, of brilliance, and I shine, but like a candle whose wick succumbs to the hot wax around it, my light is snuffed, never getting the air it needs to keep burning. I dig around the wax and pull the wick out and light it again, but what I fail to see is there is something fundamentally wrong with the candle. Maybe it is the wick? I just can't fathom the *why,* so I do not try to figure it out. I live my life with my feet planted firmly in midair. Fear's grip is especially tight as I imagine how I can manage this fork in the road, a relationship I thought was about love and the repercussions waiting for me at home. I am confused and there is not a clear path in front of me.

Bad news travels quickly. I hear Mother on the phone as I come into the kitchen. My heart beats as though it is a war drum. Her back is toward me and I tiptoe past her, but she knows I am there. I stop at the threshold between the kitchen and breakfast room to listen to the conversation.

"Try to understand? Try to understand what?"

Silence.

"She *is* young, but I don't need this right now. I can't handle this!"

Silence.

"I'll bring her in tomorrow."

She turns to me. "That's the doctor. I know all about it."

Silence.

"We're going in tomorrow for the procedure." She turns from me and picks up the phone again. She calls her sister and says, "about my daughter…"

I retreat to my bedroom and lie in darkness. The curtains are shut; long ago I stopped looking to the heavens for solace. All that remains is me, lost and sad, and I try to rationalize what is going to happen as something I can handle. But knowing myself, things will not be the same for me as they would someone else. I am weak, indecisive, a coward. "Forgive me," I say out loud to whoever or whatever hears me. I cry myself to sleep.

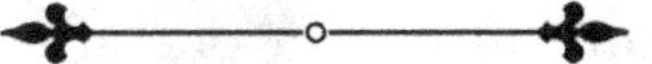

Her smile is love and her words ease my mind. "It'll be okay, when you're ready." The nurse takes my hand and walks with the gurney. I do not want to let it go.

"You'll be all right. I promise you."

"I'm not sure," I say to her as she releases my hand, bends down and hugs me tenderly.

My room has four beds and mine is next to the window. The sunshine coming through the large, rained-streaked window wakes me. The reds and yellows are a distraction, a welcome one, and I take in the colors as I sit up. Fall is my favorite time of year. School begins and I get new clothes, a hairstyle and the chance to be better. And when nature is waking up, I am winding down. School is almost done; my clothes are worn, and I need another haircut. For an instant, I think there might be something deeper there, but the thought is gone as soon as I try to focus on it.

I am not alone in my room. Two elderly women are across it and they are looking at me while whispering amongst themselves. I glance at them, filled with dread and without recourse. I get up and dress as quickly and privately as I can, though it does not dawn on me to close the bed curtain to my left. I hop, hop, hop as I put on my shoes and make my way out of the ward. *Do they know? Could they possibly know?* Their gazes follow me as I pass them, and I feel the slings and arrows of something.

The drive home is unbearable, but like everything else with this experience, I keep it all inside and endure because I deserve punishment and condemnation. "After all I've done for you," Mother begins, "This is how you repay me?" I bury my head into my chest.

"I can't believe a daughter of mine. I didn't ask anything about it. This makes me sick, and so do you." She keeps talking, but I cannot hear her clearly. Everything goes quiet and dark and my thoughts fly out of my head. For an instant, I think of Hester Prynne, how maybe she would be able to understand me, that maybe we could be friends and she could teach me how to be strong.

Mother shows up at my apartment one afternoon several weeks later with bags of new clothes from Filenes.

"You need to try these on." She hands them to me.

"Why did you buy me clothes?" I open them to find a gray suit and a few matching blouses.

"You'll need these for interviews." I do not understand since I am still an undergrad, but I comply. She tugs and pulls at the clothes until she likes the way the outfit looks.

"This color works well with the pink top. You'll need shoes at some point. I brought hangers so make sure to put everything away."

"Okay, thank you."

"Don't thank me, just show me you can be better."

I take this as a sign, a hopeful one, and after she leaves, I resolve to work harder and be someone she can be proud of, someone she wanted to be but could not.

12
Second Chance

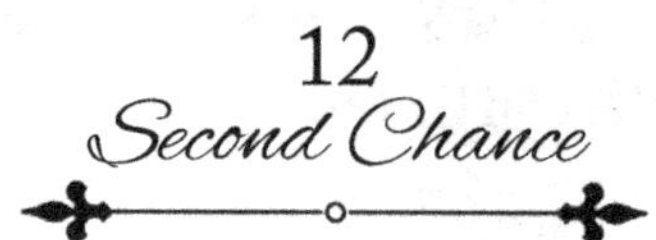

Ghostbusters is lighthearted, and my cousin and I leave the theater in good spirits, laughing and enjoying each other's company during the twenty-five-minute drive to my house. I step inside and sense something, but I am not sure what it is. The air is stale, like a hotel room for smokers, and stifling. I walk through the kitchen gingerly.

"I found them," Mother says from the top of the stairs.

"What are you talking about?"

"The pills, your birth control pills." My breath is taken away as though I opened a door expecting something pleasant, but a northeasterly wind greets me instead. I say nothing.

"I can't take this!"

"But..."

"I want you out of my house!"

I leave.

With nowhere else to go, I move in with my boyfriend. I decide to try to make the relationship work, though it has not worked for a year, and we both know it. Our bellwether was my choice to turn to Mother, and her disdain toward him is insurmountable.

"He's a waiter!"

"So? He has a job."

"Where did he go to school?"

"Does it matter?"

"Yes, what can he offer you?"

"I don't know what you're talking about."

"I know, and this is a problem. I won't ever accept this relationship, ever!'

I say nothing, try to be "happy" and make good choices, something I am not sure how to do. He concerns himself with his work and interests outside his home. I look to my sister for support, and we try to come together, but Mother's omnipresence puts a wedge between us. My brothers are out of reach, one of them telling me in a heated moment, "I hate you." I hate myself, too, so it's okay.

My mind stirs while I ride the T to Brookline. Where am I? Like a radio station whose frequency is more noise than words, there is static, and I shield myself from it because it is maddening. I walk through life surrounded by a haze. I can see out, but not clearly to understand what is happening, and no one bothers to look in since it takes too much effort; and I want someone to, but I say nothing and keep walking while life goes on all around me.

Looking out the window as the trolley makes it way along Commonwealth Avenue, the harbingers of spring are in the city: swept streets and sidewalks, people loitering about or walking briskly in lighter attire, and the small plot gardens that belong to the grand brownstones that line the avenue share their daffodils, tulips, hyacinths and crocuses with all passersby. Boston is magical in springtime. The air is clean, and since the city continues to be reborn from the spirit that sparked a revolution, it is ripe for change, which means there is always the possibility to start over. I take her in, all she has to give as a child anticipating a special birthday present.

My counselor's office is on the ground floor. A bay window casts sunlight from the north into the space. Blinds adorn the windows and are drawn halfway; though I prefer them open, I presume she wants to be mindful of my privacy and perhaps my attention, since people walk by almost continuously. A variety of plants are on the windowsill: pathos, spiders, and violets. They give the room warmth, life, and they make the place comfortable, which is important because the furniture is black leather, and the floors are bare hardwood. The walls host abstract art that is curious. I see lots of colors: reds, oranges, yellows, black, but no form that I can see. The paint is in a heap, and I suppose there is meaning in the works, but I do not know anything about this kind of art. I know nature's art, the plants and trees with their endless forms and natural color. My senses react to them without me having to do anything. But the art on the wall—I just can't quite understand it. Maybe I will someday.

I wait on the sofa while she gets a cup of tea in the kitchen. I am anxious and afraid to be here. I am twenty years old and a mess as far as I can see. I do not look like one, though, not really. I keep myself tidy and do my schoolwork. My life is quiet with a couple of girlfriends and a part-time job. It is my personal life that is in disarray. Not just my boyfriend but my family too. We are estranged, and I cannot find a way back. Honestly, sometimes I do not care, which horrifies and isolates me from myself even more.

My counselor's face is elongated, not pretty—handsome best describes its features, and her long dark hair rests on her breasts. Her posture makes her look strong, as though she overcame an obstacle with her dignity intact. As she stirs her tea and gets her notepad and pen ready, my mind churns. *Will you understand? Can you? Do we share a story? Please don't hate me for what I've done. I need help—I need someone to talk to, to help me figure all this out. I'm tired—I'm so tired of feeling shitty. Sometimes I know exactly where I'm going, but then I'm lost again. How does this happen? How can someone be together for a while and then fall apart and lose everything? I keep starting over!*

She does not smile, but she is engaged, listening to my sometimes-unproductive speech.

"What can I do for you?"

"I don't know."

"Why are you here?"

"I'm confused. I don't have control over anything."

"What does that look like?"

"Everything—my mother, my boyfriend, me, and I can't make sense."

"Of?"

"I don't know."

She waits and waits and waits for me to say something, but right beside me It has returned—Fear. I cannot bring myself to speak of the abortion, or anything, and I break down. My counselor hands me a tissue and takes notes while I churn inside again.

"Do you live with a parent?" She brings me back.

"Not anymore."

"Do you want to talk about it?"

Yes!

"What's on your mind?"

Silence.

Mother and I live on different planets. Hers revolves around jumping through specific hoops in a particular order, and this is not necessarily a bad thing. It is just not something I can live up to. I want to after all she has done for me, but I cannot find order in my world. I am suspended in space, moving on its orbit because I am compelled to do so, not because I want to. Fear assures me that it is too late for a new beginning; it is better to keep quiet and keep my troubles deep inside where I can hope to forget them. Why confront that which probably cannot be changed? This is true about the abortion, and I suppose it is true about my other issues too. I cannot get to my mother's planet, and she is not offering me a lift to hers, just expecting me to get there somehow because she has no desire to visit me where I live. So, what can I do? Nothing. My counselor reaches for me. I shrink back.

"Share with me how you want your life to be."

"Why can't things be easy?"

"What things?"

Silence.

"What things?"

I am about to cry again, and she sees this and hands me another tissue before she sits back in her chair.

"I am sorry you are in pain."

My hopes for springtime are beaten down. I retreat within to that place where I cannot be reached, and my foray into the world ends before it begins. I leave counseling after three sessions, but I take one lesson with me: it takes courage to look in the mirror.

Then something changes. After a year of silence, Mother calls me.

"It's Mom."

"Hi Mother."

"What are you doing?"

"I have a job, and I'm applying to graduate school."

"You can come home for Thanksgiving."

Silence.

"Did you hear me?"

"Yes."

"You can come home."

"Okay."

"Bye."

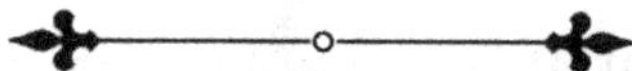

He walks in the house through the kitchen door the day before Thanksgiving, 1982. He is there with his college roommate, my sister's boyfriend. Our eyes meet; I smile; and he stares, walking until he is stopped by the kitchen cabinet. We shake hands, introduce ourselves, and go to the family room.

The house has a pulse. The television drones in the background while he and my sister's boyfriend drink, laugh and recall stories from their college exploits. My brothers join us, and it is the first time I see my older brother get drunk. I hear my mother; her house shoes tap across the linoleum floor in quick succession, from the refrigerator to the sink, and then to the stove and back to the refrigerator and then to the counter like a well-choreographed dance. She is in a good mood, which is fortuitous for me. I am brought back into the fold without question.

My sister and I take the boys to a club Friday night in Boston. My feet are numb, and New England's cold, humid air fills my spine. Chilled to the marrow, I welcome the cacophony surrounding me; though it's deafening, I warm up quickly as I share body heat with a couple hundred strangers.

"Naval aviators have beautiful children," he says, holding his glass up.

"Do they?"

The four of us spend the evening crowded in with others. He and I do not have a conversation; we exchange glances and mystery, which is enough for me, but I do wonder about him a little. He has a nice smile and a quietness that is attractive. For the time being, though, I am happy I can feel my toes again.

I pack up my stuff and leave my boyfriend's apartment a couple of months later, after he tells me he slept with a friend. I do not have a reaction for him, just resignation that this is how it is with me. There is not another way to be treated or control how I will be treated.

The sun comes out, and I make my way through the warm days in loose, comfortable clothing. Sometimes, I need a cotton sweater. My ex-boyfriend and I keep in touch; trying to make sense of us, we stumble over our words wanting to find closure, but realize there is not any, perhaps, can never be any. We just *are*, and we meet for lunch in Kenmore Square almost a year after the break-up, and he divulges that he is going to marry the woman who is carrying his child. I feign support, and I mourn again for what is lost but choose not to share my grief with him. We wish each other well before we say our last goodbye.

My graduate studies ground me. Through seminars and hands-on work in the studio, I come to understand the complexities of production, but it is the art of screenwriting that captivates me, and I dream of going to California after school to pursue it.

I am a student of film, but not just the big box office sort. These I find entertaining, and they fuel a desire to earn a lot of money, but they do not satisfy the itch I cannot scratch. From across the pond, I watch European films and find patterns: Polish cinema is politicized, its protagonists repressed, yet energized for change; Russian film is long and oppressive, even the settings are bleak, and those filmed in black and white are depressing; French film is quite entertaining, especially its romantic comedies which have a casual attitude toward sex, it is something to be enjoyed freely; British film is stoic; the rural settings are awash with splendid cottage gardens and seemingly ancient architecture that brings richness to the plot; and their actors are among the finest in the world; and Italian cinema is ingeniously creative and full of emotional characters who live from their essence. I find myself engrossed in the implausible plot of my favorite Italian film, *Swept Away*.

Its premise: Two adults from opposite worlds (northern and southern Italy) find themselves stranded on an island after a boating mishap. The northern Italian, a physically flawless and beautiful blonde woman, is lost, while the southern Italian, a rugged looking brown man with dark features, has the skills to survive. He plunges into the setting: he builds shelter and dines on shellfish he retrieves from the shoreline. You see, he has nothing to lose because his life has been one of degradation. On the island, he is free. She, on the other hand, comes from privilege and what she sees is a primitive, uninhabitable piece of earth she cannot endure. Inevitably, they reverse roles: she needs him, which consequently, empowers him.

There are a few scenes that are disturbing. The man takes advantage of his position and is cruel to the woman; in one scene, he straddles the line separating rape and rough sex, and he is verbally and physically abusive too, projecting years of frustration with the system on her. She has her moments, summoning him like a dog and tantalizing him with her naked body as though he is blind, but I see past them to the foundation of humanity and recognize the symbolism. They drop their masks, become lovers and build a life together, but paradise on Earth cannot last, and their garden of Eden is discovered, and they are rescued. Forever altered, they are compelled to return to their former lives. A tragedy. I leave the theater, after I cry through the credits, convinced I can write compelling scripts like this if given the opportunity. I dedicate myself to my studies, especially my writing, with purpose.

Mother and I co-exist without incident now that I am on my own, and my relationships with my siblings improve, especially with my younger sister. She is anxious for me to get together with him, the man I had shared nothing but a few glances with on a cold night months ago.

"He wants to see you."

"He hasn't said anything to me."

"I'm telling you, he wants to see you."

"Why can't he write?"

"He's shy."

"I don't know—"

"Come on."

Through a series of phone calls and an exchange of notes, I find myself in D.C. for the weekend at her dorm. Encouraged, I go on a double date. He and I have not exchanged "hellos" since Thanksgiving, but I trust my sister's assurances that he wants to see me.

He and his buddy drink during supper, and it persists throughout the evening. The bowling alley is sparsely populated by the time we get there later in the evening. They order a pitcher before we split into teams and bowl a set.

"I'm used to candle pins," I say.

"Candle pins? That's not bowling."

"My dad owned a bowling alley," he boasts through a wide grin that exposes a set of straight white teeth.

"Is that why you are so good?" I ask.

"I practiced a lot when I wasn't working there."

"Oh?"

"Do you know how bad the smell is when you dip pins?"

"No."

"It's awful. I hated doing that."

"What is that?"

"It keeps the pins looking good, but the chemical we used was toxic."

"That's not good."

"Sorting broken beer bottles was another nasty job I had to do."

"Sounds like it."

"And the smell—"

"At least you learned to bowl."

"Yeah, I wanted to be a pro."

"Like—what's his name? Weber?"

"Yeah."

His bowling skills dwindle as he becomes intoxicated. I sit and watch but say nothing while he and his friend carry on. Beer spills on the alley, and he decides the best way to clean it up is to pour cigarette ash on it. He scours the lanes looking for an ashtray like a pirate on a treasure hunt. He zigzags as he carries it back to our lane and keeps his eye on it as though it is gold dust.

"I know what I'm doing."

"Do you?"

"You don't think I do?"

"Doesn't make sense to me."

"The ash will absorb the beer."

He dumps the entire ashtray out and then tries to mix it in the beer, causing a mess similar to one in an open charcoal grill after rain. We are asked to leave, and I hurry him out of the door while he maintains his actions are appropriate for the situation.

"I know what I'm doing! My father owned a bowling alley!"

"Let's go," I say.

"These people don't know what they're doing!"

In the car I say nothing while he and his friend have a good laugh. "They're idiots," he says, and then all conversation ends. I agree to see him the following day alone.

The rain comes and goes as we stroll along the concrete paths of the D.C. zoo. I take it all in like a giddy schoolgirl on a field trip since it is my first visit to a zoo in years, and I take his hand and drag him around as though we have been together for a lifetime. He complies, though at times, it is clear he is not amused, especially in the bird house, which is noisy but shields us from the inclement weather.

"Do you have an umbrella in the car?"

"We don't use umbrellas in South Dakota," he says.

"What do you do in South Dakota when you're outside in the rain?"

"We deal with it."

"We use umbrellas in Boston, and since we are on the east coast, I suppose we should use one now, don't you think?" I laugh.

That evening, we ride from D.C. to Annapolis on route 50 in his Mazda RX-7. This is his prized possession, a gift from his father and mother for his academic successes, and as we race down the two-lane highway listening to Aldo Nova, the speedometer's needle shakes as it registers 90 MPH in the straightaway. The roads are slick, and I white knuckle the seat, turn my head to him, and my face pleads with him to slow down; and although he sees it, he turns up the radio, bops his head up and down and keeps going. I say nothing.

"Isn't this music great?" he says.

I grimace.

"What's wrong with you?"

"Nothing. Are we almost there?"

We stroll into McGarvey's Saloon in downtown Annapolis and sit in a dimly lit corner away from the din at the bar. We order drinks and visit.

"The Academy is a great place to be from," he says.

"Oh?" I sit up.

"It sucks while you're here."

"What do you mean?"

"The work, the rules and expectations. It's nothing like civilian schools."

"Why did you come here?"

"It's where my dad wanted me."

"Why?"

"I got into some trouble at home."

"You had no choice?"

"Once I got in, I didn't apply anywhere else."

"So, you came."

He nods, lifts his glass, and finishes his beer, still halfway full, in one gulp. "He and my mom booked a room at the Hilton and gave me money for a duck dinner before they flew me back east." He puts his pilsner down gently. "I flew in the day before I mustered."

"Alone?"

"Sure."

"What would you have done if you hadn't gotten in?"

"I thought I'd be an architect. Montana State has a program, and in the winter, I could ski."

"Did you ever consider leaving?"

"It takes courage to leave." He fiddles with his glass, picking it up, looking to the bottom of it before putting it back on the table. "At least I'll learn to fly."

The drive back to my sister's dorm puts me at ease. He leans in to kiss me goodbye and my stomach tingles. We exchange addresses. Before I go inside, I turn and watch him drive away, and I know it is the beginning of something.

My sister and her boyfriend do not last. The details of their break-up are unclear, but she is heartbroken, angry and confused. We lose touch for a while, so I am not sure how she manages. He and I continue to exchange letters while he lives in Florida, and when he invites me to my sister's ex-boyfriend's wedding, she is not pleased.

"I can't believe you're going."

"What do you want me to do?" I ask.

"Not go! Where is your loyalty?"

"Loyalty? To whom?"

"Me!"

"This isn't about you."

"Yes, it is. You don't know what he did!"

"What did he do?"

"He cheated with her!"

"Are you sure?"

"And she's pregnant!"

"He's doing what he needs to do, Sis."

"I can't believe you're going!"

"He asked me to go with him, and I want to."

"I can't stand her!"

"I want to be there to support him while he supports—"

"Don't say his name!"

"You broke up with him long before she got pregnant."

"He still cheated on me!"

"You broke up before that."

"You think you know the story, but you don't!"

"He said it was all over between you two when he met her."

"He lies!"

"I don't know what to say."

"Don't go!"

"I'm going."

"Thanks Sis, thanks a lot!"

Mother does not react to our bickering, but she does question my loyalty to the family. I defend my choice and she let it go because she wants the relationship. I fly to Atlanta where he picks me up and we travel to the wedding venue. That evening as we lie in bed, he says, "We should… you know."

I roll over and look at him. "What?"

"We should get… you know…"

"Married?"

"Yes."

"When?"

"As soon as possible."

"I need time."

"How much?"

"I don't know. Don't you want a wedding?"

"I don't care."

"My mother does."

"Okay, just soon."

From his apartment, I call Mother with the news. "We are getting married," I say.

"When?" she asks.

"I'm not sure, but I like the idea of June."

"We need a year to plan. Did you get a ring?"

"I don't want one."

"You can't be engaged without a ring."

"But I don't want one."

"You can have mine."

It feels swell to live without problems. I cannot remember being this happy since Daddy died. I am going to marry someone who loves me. Me! I look forward to the mail every day because there is usually a letter from him. Even though we do not see each other much, I know what he is doing. We talk on the phone too, sometimes for an hour, and I like this most because I hear his voice and feel his emotions coming through. I hope he feels mine and knows I love him. He is fine to let me plan everything, and he gives me money and says, "Use it to help pay for the wedding." There's just one thing: the abortion. How do I tell him about it?

I decide it is best to write a letter and share what happened. Fear is right next to me and he wants me to stay quiet, like I always do, but I cannot, not this time. I am marrying a naval officer who is honest and has integrity. He is a graduate of one of the best schools in the country, and I need to respect this. I am grateful he wants me to be his wife, so I write that he is free to walk away if he cannot live with the choice I made. Fear taps me on the shoulder as I seal the envelope, address and stamp it. To keep him at bay, I go downtown and mail the letter at the post office instead of putting it out front to be picked up by the mailman. I do not feel happy in that moment, for I dare not indulge myself just in case we are over.

He calls at the end of the week. "How are the plans going?"

"I think everything is set."

"Need anything?"

"Not right now."

"Well, let me know."

"Okay."

"Bye." He hangs up and I wait for the dial tone before I do as well.

Happiness returns.

Mother and I are in the habit of meeting for supper Friday evenings at Friendly's. There is a change in her as far as I am concerned, and I draw near to her, and it feels like what I imagine a mother and daughter relationship is when there are no obstacles to overcome. She supports my choices without judgement and counsels me without the guilt, and I think we have made it; we have crossed over to the other side, and I believe the words she said to me years ago, "I prayed for a daughter with blue eyes, and here you are!"

His mother chimes in also, which I welcome, and she contributes her ideas for the celebration at Mass. We discuss music and protocol for the sacrament through letters. From the inception of our relationship, his mother has been a presence in my life. As Mother puts it, "She courted you too." She approves of me, of us, and she heralds me into the family as "the girl back East." His grandmother is a bit put off when she finds out I am Italian, and he and I laugh it off because my grandmother has similar sentiments about his Irish background. She is adamant I change my name, as is he.

"I like my name."

"But we'll be married."

"It's all I have left of Daddy."

"You will be my wife, and what about the children?"

"They can have your name."

"But it will be different than yours."

"So?"

I do not like the tension between us, and I do not want to displease my grandmother, so I acquiesce. Because of my work we decide to go west, and we can because he graduates at the top of his class, but through a series of bureaucratic mishaps, he receives orders to the East coast. With the stroke of a pen from a cog in a wheel, my aspirations fade away like the final scene in a movie you do not want to end.

"I can try to get the orders reversed, but it'll mean my buddy loses his."

"Will it work?"

"I'm not sure, not likely."
"Oh."
"Are you okay?"
"I wanted—"
"I don't know what I can do."
"It'll be fine."
"Are you sure?"
"Yes."
"They say Virginia is for lovers."
Silence.
"Did you hear me?"
"Yes."
"Well…"
"Well, it is a good thing we are lovers."
"Yes, it is."

13

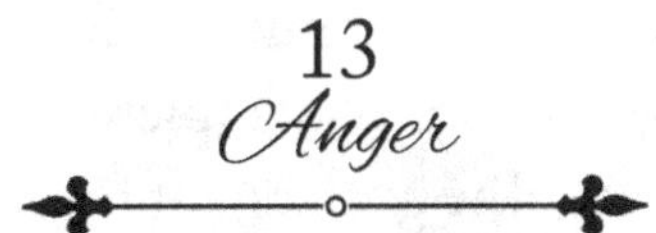

Anger

I have come to understand that divorce follows a grieving process; even though I know it is best to leave my marriage, I do not foresee the emotional ordeal involved in its dissolution. I am sad, lost and contemplative much of the time, milling about wearing a mask, but lately, I am plagued by anger, and it consumes all the other emotions within as a forest fire does to all in its destructive path. Its wake leaves desolation and charred remains unrecognizable to those who behold it, and it comes from a deep place within one's being unbeknownst to the soul; there it resides, fermenting, cogitating and waiting patiently for a moment to strike. I am caught off guard and am at its mercy.

The "what ifs" and "if onlys" are battling each other. My mind is a boxing ring, and these two questions are like heavyweight boxers in a championship bout. With nowhere to go, I seek respite in the attic among the boxes that define my life.

A drawstring hangs down from a retractable staircase, and I have to jump, jump, jump but still cannot grasp it. "Shit!" I do not have the energy or desire to get the step ladder in the pantry, so the stool in the laundry room will have to do, though it is wobbly.

The attic light is accessible from the top rung, and I stretch and stretch until I reach the chain and turn it on. I am swamped by it all, even though I know what to expect. I massage my thighs with the palms of my hands, as though I just completed a marathon, because I notice several empty plastic containers and one five-gallon bucket in the back, under the vents. *I hope you sealed them before you left!*

Earlier, I looked beyond the foundation plants out front to the fifty-foot gutter than ran the expanse of the front of the house. It is in trouble. The portion above the garage is almost completely detached from the eave. Three spikes hold it in place. The gutters out back are in trouble and barely holding on as well. Two small gutters are in a side bed, yanked from their eaves a couple of years ago during a nor'easter, while another in dappled shade has morphed into a planter for vagrant seeds. The front railings are rotted at their bases, and I noticed many of the slats supporting the porch railing are rotted too. The 6x6s look good as far as I can tell. Much of the paint on the trim is peeled away exposing bare wood to the elements, and the side door to the garage is rusted through and falling off its hinges while the back door cannot be opened at all because it is swollen. There is mold on the roof, house and back deck, which is also rotted in some places. These are the chores… chores he said he'd get to but never does, then suggests I do them and I do not, though I painted the trim out front many years ago; although I implore him to let me hire someone, he refuses, and this indifference causes the house to deteriorate. Yet, I am still expected to cook, clean, and keep his life sorted because he says, "It's the least you can do since I make more money." Now, all this is my responsibility, and he has the gall to say, "You're getting more with this house than I'm getting with my living arrangement so stop your whining." Asshole! It will cost thousands to get this house fixed.

I open a large box filled with scuba gear. Inside, I see the quarry and campsite. He encourages me to learn to dive so we have something to do together. I enroll, pass a written exam, and then go away for a weekend with him to take the practical test.

"I passed." I change into comfortable clothing before I hang up my wet suit outside our tent and put my gear away. This is a nice place, clean, fresh water, nice campsite. I had no idea this was here.

"After we eat, I'm going to hang out with some other divers by their campfire," he says.

"It's my birthday."

"I won't be long, just a few beers."

"Please don't."

"I'll be back."

He leaves after we eat, and I listen to him laugh, drink and carry on with strangers until I fall asleep. I mention the incident in the morning, but he is abrupt. "Quit it, it was just a few beers." I close the box with a snap, and I sit back on my heels, numb.

His promises, the words I accepted as gospel, written to me in a desperate plea to keep our engagement have been duds. They showed promise at first but fizzled out just when they needed to burst into color. I wanted to admire his seemingly committed demeanor, but I cannot. All I experience is disappointment. I plow the box to the stairs only to find the boat cushions and matting behind the HVAC unit. "Fuck it! This was your job to take care of! It never changes, never! You do as you please knowing I will pick up the slack and shit—I'm doing it!" I throw all the cushions and matting down the stairs.

He drinks whenever he can through the years, either alone or with buddies he picks up along the way. Even after the birth of our first, he insists on going out without me and our daughter on weekends to party. One evening he comes home with several friends and raids the pantry. I awake to the commotion and hurry downstairs to break it up before she is disturbed. I find one young man lining my window boxes with Oreos. "What are you doing!" He says, "Just making it look nice."

"Get them out of here! She's asleep and it's late—after midnight!"

He says, "Relax, we just had a few beers."

"Now!" I insist. A smart-ass friend turns to him and says, "She's going to heaven and you're going to hell." They both laugh as he escorts everyone to their cars.

He curbs his outings for many years after this episode, choosing to stay home and drink while I tend to the children until he meets another drinker. In the two or so years we are stationed with him, he is back in a familiar routine. One morning I find he has not been to bed, and when I look out a window and see his truck, I race through the house looking for him. Almost frantic, I grab the phone to call his friend when I realize he is outside sleeping on the diving board located at the deep end of our pool. I go to our daughters' room and make sure they are asleep and the blinds are closed before I approach him.

"Get up!" I nudge him. "Get up! I don't want the girls to see you!"

"Whaaat?"

"Where have you been! Oh, never mind! Just get up and go to our bed!"

"Just had a few beers, what's your problem?"

I breathe in and breathe out. Why is it the marriage I wanted was always a few beers away?

After a few years his interest in diving ends, like his other interests in our thirty years together. He spends years trying to keep himself entertained. Downstairs, a polluted 55-gallon aquarium waits for me, forsaken by him over a year ago. This is the last of several tanks in our life, and I indulge his interest for several years, but his desire to keep a viable ecosystem is abandoned at the same time he completely withdraws from our life. The garage is filled with woodworking tools: drill press, table saw, band saw, jig saw, planer, saw blades, drill bits and chisels—most of it in disrepair. There is a small collection of rusted hand tools as well. He flirts with the notion of making furniture for several years, and I encourage him. We shop for plans, tools, and wood together, and he makes a few nice pieces for our home. About five years later, he quits for no apparent reason. The garage is also home to his fishing equipment: poles and tackle boxes, and camping gear: tents, sleeping bags, and supplies. All this stuff he leaves behind, years' worth of leisurely pursuits which keep his attention for short bursts of time.

There are other brief preoccupations along the way: skeet shooting, home brewing, models, and trains; at first, we share these activities, but they always get boring to him and subsequently are abandoned.

"I'm leaving thousands of dollars' worth of stuff," he reminds me one afternoon.

"Thousands of dollars we could have used for our children or for us!" I quip.

"Quit your whining."

What a prick. He whines constantly about his life, the lack of money and people in it who aren't idiots. And what do I do? I listen to him and sort through it and buffer him from the children and make sure he has what he wants so he can be happy for once in his fucking life! We agree to take care of our personal belongings, but like so many other times, his promises are lies. I turn the light off and climb down the attic stairs. I forget about the boat mats and cushions I dropped from it, and when I see them on the floor I yell, "Fuck you, and Fuck him!"

I stomp down the hall only to halt at the threshold of what was once our bedroom. He has poisoned it for me, and a burning sensation wells up before it erupts from my mouth. "Motherfucker! No respect, not for our home, or me! You've destroyed everything! What a fucking mess!" I turn around and stomp down the stairs to the pantry and with a jerk, pluck a large black garbage bag from the pantry. The box falls to the floor and I leave it there.

I snap the garbage bag and it fills with air like a windsock on a brisk fall day, and with a swift up and down motion, it opens wide. "All of this is gone, dickhead!" I start in the closet, picking up small piles of discarded clothes left on the floor. I take those draped on their hangers and they spin and fall to the floor. I snatch them and shove them into the bag too. It tears. "You motherfucking prick!" I shove the sullied, discolored bed sheets and blanket into the bag. Pieces of paper, wrappers and military insignia litter the carpet, left behind like remnants of a concert. I bend over, dragging the bag behind, and as I pick up each bit, I spit the words out like I'm spewing poison.

"You shithead, rat bastard! Even as you leave, I hate you. Hate, hate, hate you for doing this to me, for leaving it all behind for me to figure out!" I peek inside the bathroom, "What the fuck! I can't do this, not today!"

Down the stairs I go, but an adrenaline rush trips me up. I grab hold of the railing and look up to the ceiling.

"I don't want this! Do you hear me? Do you?" I sit down, let go of the bag and bury my face in my hands. "You're not worth my tears! I was a good wife, damn you! I fucking loved you through it all!" And then his words, "Stop whining, you have it good," invade my space, and I'm back in the moment with him.

"I know I have it good."

"Then stop your whining."

"Can't you spend time with me? A hug? A kiss?"

"I'm busy, woman."

I shake my head to bring myself back to the present. "Get out of there... leave now!" I get up and take the garbage to the curb.

There, along with an assortment of "stuff" he had to own, I toss the bag. His legacy is trash. These are the remains of another life. The bags are piled high, at least four feet, and I marvel at the complete and total irony in this picture.

No more! Never again will I make money an issue in my life. I spent years worrying there was never enough, told we would never have wealth, never have "things" we could afford, reminded there would not be enough to retire if I didn't "change my ways". Shit, we had plenty of money. It was your attitude toward it that kept us from enjoying it, and your mindset kept us in relative poverty. And I let you! What the fuck was I thinking? And then you tell me I'll be bankrupt in two years after you leave. Your arrogance makes me sick! Bullshit! Total bullshit!

"I need to get rid of the bedroom set." The words come out before my brother-in-law says, "Hello?"

"Oh?" he says.

"I'm going to sell it or give it away. I don't care. I can't have it here anymore!"

"Your mother's set?"

"Yes, it has to go. I can't take it!"

"Okay, sweetie."

"Will you take it?"

"Where will I put it, hon?"

"I don't know—I'll just sell it."

"Your mom will be upset."

"I don't care. I need this set out of my life. I don't want any reminder!"

"Settle down, hon, settle down."

"I can't believe this is my life! Who leaves it all behind like this?"

"I can't answer your question."

"I'm left to clean up our life."

"It'll be fine."

"When? When will it be fine? He didn't skip a beat. I feel like a dupe!"

"It's not your fault."

"He didn't love me!"

"We love you."

"Will you take the set?"

"I don't think we need it."

"I just have to get rid of it!"

"Don't get rid of it, we'll take it."

"Thank you."

I move the two nightstands and two dressers to the far side of the bedroom. They crowd in the corner as recalcitrant children do. I take the bed frame apart and lean it against the wall along with the mattress and box springs. I vacuum until the cannister fills to capacity, and after I empty it. I put the kettle on.

As I watch the birds at the feeders, I am reminded of a story I have heard over the years while at Mass. Jesus teaches his disciples the birds of the air do not toil, reap or store in barns, yet the Creator feeds them. I know that God values me more than birds, and this knowledge fills me with warmth, as if a comforter is wrapped around me in an embrace.

Despite my efforts to keep it together, my marriage is over and so is that embrace. Divorce is counterintuitive to the Church; it is a direct assault on its foundation. Jesus tells us, "Whoever divorces his wife and marries another, commits adultery against her; and if she divorces her husband and marries another, she commits adultery." There is no place to go! Who am I without the Church? My inner light retreats and hides itself under a bush, and my still quiet voice goes mute. There are no comforting words after the end, the penitential rite cannot offer me a clean slate.

I loved with all my heart, mind, and soul. I offered my children to you—I brought them up at your altar. I received the sacraments, and I lived my life as your servants advised to keep my marriage blessed. I prayed and consecrated myself to the Blessed Mother. I adorned my chest with her scapula, convinced my devotion would fortify not only me but him too, uplifting our marriage for a greater purpose until it was time for us. I imitated those souls who came before and suffered. I tolerated the dismissiveness, the unkind words, and the lack of empathy in my marriage. I persevered through the inconsistencies in the teachings of The Church too, and I accepted my role as a Catholic woman. I defended the successors of Peter while the Church struggled in darkness, its shame revealed in the light. I'm in darkness now, the darkness of a moonless night at sea. Where are you, my guiding light? How will I find my way back to shore? I wait, but it is no use. There is no sign—nothing but a dark, empty space that hums like a refrigerator.

Echoes of "God's righteousness" bounce off the walls in my mind. And then a thought, an epiphany in a way, but a sad one which brings heartache and grief. I say to the birds, "Is my faith in the Church and sacraments the source for meaning in this life, or just a collection of notions espoused to keep me in submission?" The kettle whistles; it startles me, but I pour. Anger percolates while my tea steeps. "God does not feed the birds—I do!"

Three weeks pass, and I learn one morning that my positive state of well-being is a Trojan horse.

"How could you? Who is she to ride my bike, sit on my seat and use my pedals? Who is she to intrude in my place?" I sit in front of my computer screen. A hot flash blurs my vision. "I knew it!" I replay the video I find on her Facebook page. My heartbeat quickens with each replay. "Are you on interstate 91? Heading to Sturgis? Must be. That's when we rode the interstate. I know you! It was March. I saw you on my feed with my brother-in-law. You were both drunk and you spoke to me, so I spoke to him."

"Do you know this woman?" I point.

"Yes." He steps back.

"She looks like someone you'd hookup with."

"She smokes."

"She might quit for you."

"You met her at a party while visiting your ailing father? Could it have been sooner? Could this be why you were angry and hostile when you returned from your trips? What's been going on, huh? You are a liar, cheat, and a fraud! Fuck you! Here you are, riding with her like it's innocent, a chance meeting, serendipitous. I know better, all too well in fact, that I have been replaced like a dead battery or worn tire. My ride through the hills is hers now. Thirty fucking years and you turn the page without even reading the words. You walked away years ago and forgot to tell me, you pathetic small man!" His prophetic words come back to me. "It takes courage to leave."

I replay the video. You and she exchange smiles. Yours, reflected in the side mirror, she records for the virtual world to see. She turns the camera to herself and shares her anticipation. I want to throw up, spew all over whatever of his I can find lying around the house. I get up quickly, knocking the kitchen table chair over. I shoo it away with my foot.

In the garage, I open the cabinets and throw their contents on the floor and kick them about.

"No, no, no, no! I didn't let this happen! I didn't! I don't want to see—I don't want to see any of this! Fuck! I gave him thirty years, everything!"

Pacing in a circle, my body heat rises until I want to explode, but I do not. I implode.

"I wanted you and tried to lure you back. How did I become so very undesirable?" I yearn for tears to relieve the anguish, as a cool compress on the forehead relieves a temperature, if only temporarily. I go limp, my energy drains and collects on the garage floor as I melt down. On my knees and trembling, the truth reveals itself. "You'll marry her."

I retreat to my butterfly garden, but I do not know which way to turn. My torso tries to lead my legs, first twisting right, then left, but my legs do not budge because my knees are locked.

How could I have not seen this coming? Why didn't I see us? Did you? Is this why you were ill at ease? I clench my fists. *Is this why you resented the lifestyle you chose for us?* Tighter. *Is this why you had sand in your shoes?* Tighter. *Was your restlessness the reason you whipped me with words, ignored my identity, and vanquished my value? Shit!* I release my fists, cover my face with my hands. *Where the hell have I been?* I was there.

Panicked, perplexed and paranoid, I make a desperate call.

"Can you get on Facebook?" I ask.

"Give me a minute," my sister-in-law says. "Where am I going?"

"This is the name."

"Who is this?"

"Her."

"When?"

"He said he's known her since January, but I'm not sure that's true."

"Who is she?"

"I don't know."

"Are you okay?"

"No, I'm not."

"Hold on, here's his brother."

"How are you?" he asks.

"Confused."

"I want you to know that we love you and you'll always be family."

"No, we won't. He'll marry her."

"We don't know this."

"He will! He can't take care of himself—he needs help!"

"I think I know my brother."

"No! You don't know him!"

"I hear what you're saying."

"You don't hear! Help him, please help him!"

"I'm trying to understand you, but you need to calm down."

"He lied to me. He lied to me!" Out of the corner of my eye, I see them on Facebook.

"I'm not taking sides."

"I called you years ago about his drinking! No one listened, no one!" I play the video. "It's not right! We're still married! No respect, none!"

"I hate social media for this reason."

"It brought them together."

"You don't know this."

"I have my suspicions."

"I can't talk to you like this."

"Then don't!" My hands shake, "He lied about us! Lied to me! The family!"

"I'm not taking sides. I haven't spoken to him."

"I can't do this! I can't do this!"

"I don't understand."

"Of course, you don't. Have you ever understood? Has anyone on this side of the family ever taken a fucking look at what is going on all around them?"

"I hear you and you will always be my sister."

"It's over!" I hang up.

I am obsessed with them and their new life together. So is Anger, and he and I seek revenge. We want him to suffer for treating me poorly and not wanting to live his life with me. We need him to feel intense pain because his control issues defined our marriage as a legal agreement with specific roles instead of a partnership based on tenderness and acceptance. He lied too, something he berated me about throughout our marriage and punished me over one evening in the second year of marriage.

It was the evening before a friend's wedding. I am evasive about spending money, fearing reprisal. He catches me and for an instant, I wish to be a better liar. I sit and wait for his judgement, again, and it is okay because I am not completely honest and having the desire to be a skilled liar is reprehensible.

He looks for the album methodically, slowly; and once he takes it from its sleeve, dusts it off and lays it on the turntable, he places the needle at just the right spot and turns up the volume full blast. The lyrics assault me: "Liar, liar, liar." Frozen in place, I sit and absorb them while he stands over me. He plays the words again and again until I run upstairs and shut the bedroom door. *Three Dog Night* is ruined for me.

All this anger toward him does not make me feel better, and what is worse, it does not impact him. After all, he has this new life. He looks happy surrounded by her and new friends. He is at the lake, or he is out at a bar, or at a concert. He starts a new life, and I am his patsy. Filled with Anger and so many emotions, I message him.

"I saw it."

"Saw what?"

"The two of you on our bike."

"You saw a picture?"

"On Facebook."

No response.

"You didn't waste any time finding a new drinking buddy." My fingers bang out on the keyboard.

"I moved on."

"She was there all along in the back of your mind. No wonder it was easy for you to move on." My fingers tremble as I text. "You lied. Everything I did to leave our marriage was to help you."

No response.

"I am heartbroken. I gave all I had to you and the children and you let it go, for this?"

"You never listened to me. You didn't appreciate my role in the relationship."

"What does this mean?"

"You kicked me to curb, so yeah, I moved on."

"I didn't do that! I couldn't get near you, and you didn't want to help us."

"You're happy to take my retirement."

"Our retirement. I earned my twenty percent."

"You did well by me."

"I helped you. Your success was mine too."

"Maybe you'll find true love and won't live off me anymore."

"I stood by you, raised your children and loved you! Isn't that true love?"

"I found someone who truly loves me. And she doesn't irritate or annoy me."

Something pierces my gut. "Don't compare me to her."
We exchange several more texts over many weeks but end up nowhere.
"You don't communicate," he says.
"I tried."
"You're dishonest. You didn't tell me what was going on."
"I took care of our life while you were away! I didn't keep secrets!"
"You did what you wanted. You didn't think of me."
"I thought of you and the children. We were good parents. The kids turned out well."
"They had my influence."
Silence.
"The kids would be fine with her, but you poison the water."
"You put your relationship all over Facebook!"
Silence.
"How do you do it?" I ask.
"What?"
"Forget!"
"There's nothing to remember."

14
Patterns

I stretch to the right, raising my arms and interlocking my fingers. I hold the pose while the water massages my neck; then I move to the left, holding the stretch, massaging the other side, as my mind recounts the day in the garden.

The Vinca is finally filling the bed, and the rhododendron is going to make it after many iffy years. I'll have to remember to tell Glen next time I see him at the garden center. The bog garden needs a path to the feeder and the sea oats need to be divided. I hope they take off— it's an easy plant and the noise it makes as the winds blows through it reminds me of Cape Cod. If only an ocean were nearby—heaven. I wonder if the pickerel weed will spill over into it? Mixed with the arum it would look nice; the white and blue flowers blending together would add more color after the Siberian iris finishes its bloom; and the copper iris is triple its size in two years! Its blooms—like a fistful of pennies strewn about the bog. Love it and no maintenance. I need to buy more natives, definitely. It didn't take long for the butterfly garden to be overrun with mint. Do I kill it? I need to do something before it overtakes the Echinacea and Coreopsis. I'll try to dig it out first. And I need to weed the crevices in the driveway. How do they find those, year in and year out? As I shave my legs, underarms, and scrub myself clean, I am satisfied even though my work in the garden is never finished or the work I do on myself.

Sharon and I speak a lot about patterns of behavior that are difficult to discern in real time. I enjoy routine, nothing stringent, but a general course of action that is predictable. For me, it helps keep my mind clear; and an uncluttered mind is at peace. For years, I fell into patterns of behavior I thought were typical given my life's experiences, but this was not the case, and Sharon encourages me to review them, and so I do while I ready for our session later in the day. They stay with me until she and I work through them.

The sheets are clean, and I settle in and wait for him. The sound of water arouses me from slumber, but I do not open my eyes. I listen as he walks across the front of our bed. He bumps into it before he pauses at his dresser. He steadies himself and then walks to his side and climbs in. Waiting for him, I lie still, but I extend my legs to let him know I am there. Nothing. It has been months since we have been intimate. He has told me many times I need to lose weight, though not directly, and this must be the issue. I know I am not where I was, so I join a gym.

"You did what?"

"Joined the Y."

"How much?"

"Fifty-five a month."

"You better go. If you don't, I'm canceling your membership. You didn't discuss this with me."

"I thought you'd be pleased."

"We'll see."

My current nickname is Slim, and it replaces my enduring name, Woman, whenever I reach for a snack.

"Hey Slim, do you think you should eat that brownie?"

I end up sneaking it when he is not around, so I don't have to answer the question. He calls me Slim when he is annoyed too, but not necessarily at me.

"These people are idiots!"

"What do you mean?"

"They have no idea how to manage—none."

"It's not the military. Maybe in time…"

"What do you know, Slim?"

He calls me Verne throughout the early years of marriage. I do not know why except that he gets a kick out of the Marva Maid guy, Ernest, who refers to a mystery man named Verne in TV commercials. Ernest is a bit of a dolt, but he thinks the ads are funny and decides Verne is who I am.

"Know what I mean, Verne?"

"Please, enough is enough. Why are you doing this?"

"What do you mean, Verne?"

"Please call me by my name."

"I'm just kidding," he says. "What's your problem?"

"I want to be called by my name."

"Okay, Verne." He laughs.

Church Lady, another moniker he adopts from TV, eventually wins out to Verne, and I live with it for many years.

"What do you know? Oh, that's right, you're the Church Lady."

"That isn't a compliment."

"It's what you are."

"Because I'm raising the children in the Church?"

"You just are a Church Lady."

"Stop! I have a name."

"Yeah, Church Lady."

Silence.

"I'm just kidding! What's your problem?"

He settles on Woman.

"Woman, where are my keys?"

"Down here in the family room."

"Woman, did you do laundry?"

"Everything is clean and put away."

"I can't find any socks, Woman."

"You probably left them under the sofa."

"Well that's not good is it, Woman?"

"I'll get them."

And so it goes for nearly ten years now. I have not heard him say my name unless he is talking to his family on the phone, and this does not happen often.

Still waiting for him, he does not stir, and my body aches for connection. Our words fail us a lot at this point, but maybe, just maybe, we can come together without words. With his back to me, my hand hovers over his shoulder. I rest it there before I kiss it.

The jolt from his elbow as it slams into my gut sends me to my side of the bed in an instant. There, I curl into the fetal position, wrapping my legs up under my nightgown and then wrapping my arms around my legs. A surge of heat surrounds me like a defense shield, and yet, I shiver as though it is a winter's night and I am without cover. My body cries out for attention, and I hear her plea.

I escape with her to another place where the fantasy plays out as it did so many times while he was away. It has not changed after thirty years; it is still fresh, crisp and hopeful of what can be, if only. I try to take her there to feel the pleasure she cannot remember. My hand moves, and there are no rolls, wrinkles, or blemishes. There is long dark hair and a toned brown body. She does not respond. *Harder? Do I need to try harder?* She explains that we cannot go back, not anymore because Reality will not let us, at least it will not let her. I take my hand away and tighten my hold on us.

"There are patterns," Sharon says. "Do you see them?"

"Patterns?"

"Yes, throughout your marriage. What were you just thinking about?"

"Moments that stick out."

"And what do they tell you?"

"I was on my own through the years I was married." I nestle myself into the recliner.

"What did it feel like?"

"Isolation and profound loneliness, even though we shared a home life and a bed."

"What did it look like?"

"Nick names I didn't like but endured and very little affection, none in the last three years of our marriage. I waited for him. I hoped that he would see me and rescue me from my loneliness, but he didn't. In the last few years, if I got too close to him in bed, he'd push me back to my side. He elbowed me one time."

"What did you do?"

"I'd curl up and turn away from him. He didn't want to sit near me either when he was in the family room, so I didn't go in it. We even got to the point where he traveled by himself to our son's sporting events, if he went."

"How else?"

"We didn't share thoughts or feelings. He told me early on he didn't want to hear about my problems because that was what my sister was for."

"What did you do?"

"I turned to my sister or a friend, but mostly, I kept to myself and tried to work it out through prayer and communion with the saints."

"Anything else?"

"It's hard to know. He told me things, disseminating information he thought I needed, nothing personal unless he was drunk, but even then, he told a story. He didn't share. I don't get it, Sharon, but I want to."

"His stories aren't your stories. They may give insight in time, but for now, you need to focus on you."

"I think he tried to do for the children in ways things weren't done for him, and there were times I buffered them from him, but when it came to us, nothing. He was mostly just angry toward me, as if I was to blame for everything."

"Why was it different for you?"

"I don't know. He didn't see me as someone to hold on to."

"You understand you're not to blame."

"That's not how it played out."

"You can't let his perceptions affect you, not anymore. As I've said, you and he have different vibrations."

"I was his wife. I was supposed to be his closest friend, but I felt like I was the problem."

"You are not to blame."

"But I can't stop thinking I may be."

"You've digested his words for years now. It'll take some time to flush them from your body."

Silence.

"Do you see the abandonment?"

"What do you mean?"

"Your loneliness was brought about because you felt he abandoned you. He wasn't there, not on an emotional level because of where he was. The question is, is your grief from the abandonment in the marriage, or is it ongoing?"

"Grief?"

"Yes, but let's put that aside for now. Is your feeling of abandonment ongoing?"

"Ongoing?"

"Yes, have you felt abandoned before, in childhood or adolescence?"

"I did when Daddy died."

"I understand. But the abandonment is your perception, not your father's intention."

"Cancer took him, but I never got over his death. I am fatherless."

"He's with you."

"I know he is, but I don't feel him anymore."

"But you did?"

"Oh yes, many times over the years."

"What a blessing."

"I thought so too, but it's been so long."

"I feel him now." Sharon coughs and clears her throat. "He says, you're my brave girl."

"I was his brave girl, but not anymore, not in years."

"He's smiling."

"Can you ask him why he left me?"

Sharon listens and nods her head. "He didn't want to be here long. The cancer came from exposure to chemicals during the war. This is how he got out of this life early."

"He chose his path?"

"We all do."

"What does he look like?"

"His eyes are very blue, powerfully blue."

"I remember those from my wedding."

"He wants you to listen to the people helping you. He wants you to trust their guidance."

Silence.

"Let's go to the table."

"You don't talk much about your mother," Sharon says after a moment.

"Oh?"

"You bonded with your dad on this plane, and your relationship beyond this world is strong too, but what about your mother?"

"Our relationship isn't easy."

"Why?"

"I couldn't get close to her."

"What does that mean?"

"She wasn't available. She was a good provider and a responsible mother, but she wasn't a friend or someone I could talk to. She was distant."

"And now?"

"She supports me from a distance and it's all good. She didn't have it easy and she didn't give up. She soldiered on; she taught me fortitude and perseverance."

"Sounds like you've made peace with her."

"For the most part. I have a ways to go, but I'll get there. She is an excellent grandmother."

"She's in a better place."

"I hope so."

"There are patterns in all our lives, some are not useful. It's your task to find those and reshape them."

"How would you define abandonment?"

"What do you mean?"

"Do you think abandonment is just a physical thing?"

"I think it's physical and emotional."

"What does it look like emotionally?"

"You mentioned a lack availability. I think it can look like that. Why?"

"I'm trying to grasp the idea of it."

"You have a lot to process, so don't force anything. This idea along with other patterns will reveal themselves."

I close my eyes as the Tibetan music whisks me away to another plane. There, I see the shackles again, but this time, I see them clearly: they are the patterns that define my marriage. I let go and they play out.

It is the first time we have been out to eat in six years. Last time, the occasion was his promotion. This time it is because my son made the JV baseball team, but something else needs to be celebrated as well.

"I am Teacher of the Year."

"You?" he says.

"Me!"

"Congratulations, Mom."

"Thanks, honey."

"Why you?" he says.

"I'm not sure, but I'm happy about it."

"How many teachers are there?"

"I don't know, maybe forty or forty-five. Why?"

"Huh, you. Teacher of the Year. Ready to order, Dude?"

I sit there looking at him while he scans the menu. I work with many teachers deserving the honor too, but his behavior is odd, and it does not hit me why until after I butter a piece of bread. It is stale, like his words: "What's so hard about what you do? You teach retards all day."

"Did you enter all your receipts?" he says one evening.

"Yes."

"Have you balanced the checkbook?"

"Yesterday."

"Is it balanced to the penny?"

"It's fifty cents off."

"Did you find the difference?"

"No."

"Did you look?"

"I did, but I can't find it. I checked all the entries twice, fees, deposits…"

"It's got to be there. It balanced last month?"

"To the penny."

"Then…"

"I didn't see it. Maybe we missed a fee, added one too many?"

"I don't know, but you're fine to hit the happy button and be done instead of being thorough. That's why we have no money and won't be able to retire. You need to change your ways, Woman."

"It's okay."

"Of course it is for you, a liberal artist."

"Please don't."

"A mind is a terrible thing to waste."

His presence is all around me, and I cannot make decisions without its influence. The children need clothes, supplies for school, and there are fees for activities too. He is away for six months cruising, but I waffle, and I go back and forth when they ask me for money or things. I am scared and weak, and I see his face and hear his words: "What are you doing? Why are you spending money? Have we talked about it?" We banter, but I succumb, or I ignore the voice and do as I please, knowing I'll feel the ramifications of my decisions when he gets home.

"I see what you spend."

"I know."

"You spent a lot on clothes."

Silence.

"Did you save?"

"Yes."

"Not enough, I'm sure."

"And these activities?"

"The girls like them."

"Swimming lessons I get, but the rest they don't need. Got it?"

Silence. "Got it?"

"Yes."

His presence restrains me, like a strait jacket, and I let it control me too. When new vacation spots and visits to my family come up, he ignores them because they are not important to him. What is important to him is control over the course of our life, and I trust that his actions come from a place of love, a desire to share with our children what makes him happy. So we spend our free time in South Dakota visiting his family and enjoying what the Black Hills has to offer, and I figure his lack of interest in my family and the beauty of New England is okay. At least the children enjoy the visits and have fond memories. Life proceeds and it is not all bad; it is just not mine most of the time. I am a wife and mother, and these roles suffice. There is no person, only Woman.

"What is it?" Sharon asks after she chimes the bells.

"The patterns, I see them." I sit back in the recliner.

"Oh?"

"I am not enough just as I am. I haven't been for years. I thought this was a recent thing, but I was wrong. How did this happen?"

"What else do you see?"

"He is always there, even when he is away, and I can't make a move without him. When I do, I'm in trouble. I think I gave up and let him control me a long time ago and lived with it."

"How do you feel?"

"Angry, really pissed off at him."

"I see. Anything else?"

"I wasn't me, not really, because I tried to be what he wanted so he would be happy. I am tired, have been so tired with his being pissed—and then not pissed at me for whatever. I didn't know where I stood."

"Now that you know what has been, you can adjust and move forward."

Silence.

"How do you feel now?"

"As though a door has closed but a window has opened."

That evening, while I sit in the quiet on my sofa, I think about Daddy and my love for him. I lean back against the sofa, teacup cradled in my hand. *I will always see you through the prism of a wide-eyed eight-year-old girl, Daddy, as it should be.* Peace is behind me, leaning against the back of the sofa, her ease spilling down my back.

15
Seeking

He comes from a family rooted in Catholicism, and soon enough I understand I am expected to raise our children in the faith. Committing myself to the Church and attending Mass weekly at Saint Brigid after we are engaged is like visiting with an old friend: there is a familiarity, an opportunity to reacquaint with her mysteries and traditions. I have finally come home to the Church, but I have unfinished business that can no longer wait, and when we are stationed in California, before I receive the Sacrament of Confirmation, I gather my courage and do what I need to do.

"Forgive me father for I have sinned. It has been twenty-one—no, twenty-two years since my last confession."

Father Peter smiles at me, the green in his eyes twinkling like an emerald under a spotlight in a glass case.

"What is bothering you?" He leans in. Inhaling, I unburden. "I'm going through the sacrament of Confirmation soon."

"Wonderful, and whose name have you chosen?"

"Ruth."

"Ruth?"

"Yes, father."

"This is unconventional. Why?"

"Her goodness, her loyalty and willingness to serve."

"We have many saints who've done that."

"She speaks to me."

He smiles. "What is it you're carrying?"

My eyes downcast, I say, "I had an abortion."

"I see." He takes my hands. "God loves you, and so do I."

"Am I lost?"

"No, you are found."

I look up. "What do I do now?"

"Offer a Mass for the one."

Silence.

"Let's pray. Heavenly father, look down on your daughter and grant her peace. I absolve you in the name of the Father, the Son, and the Holy Spirit. Go on your way and sin no more."

I drive home but do not remember how I get there; and as I tuck my daughters in that evening, I am overcome with love for them. In the shower later that night I cry, and the tears come from a place I cannot name; and they blend with water and soap to cleanse my body and soul. The journey begins.

I choose to align with Saint Louis-Marie Grignion de Monfort, a French priest and confessor, after I read his collection of writings about the Blessed Mother. She is a humble woman, willing to submit to the will of God; yet she is not weak-minded or impressionable; she possesses her truth.

Reading, praying, and meditating over several weeks, I prepare myself for consecration; it is a joyful adventure I keep to myself... *In the presence of all the heavenly court, I choose thee this day for my mother and mistress.* I wear St. Dominic's scapula, a reminder of my love and devotion to her example. With her, I embrace unconditional love, authenticity, the simple path to holiness. She lets me in as if I were a child who peeks behind a door past her bedtime and is seen by an adoring parent.

A dozen red roses lay at the base of a wooden statue of the Blessed

Mother; she humbly accepts the offering. Her presence palpable, I stand back, take in the energy, and heed her direction. *Look to Him, always to Him first. He is the Way. I follow behind.* I say, *I love you. Help me with my children, please, dear mother.* Her warmth refreshes me like a morning shower, and with her hand on my back she guides me, as a mother who urges her hesitant child forward, and she nurtures me so I can nurture my children.

Hail Mary full of grace, the Lord is with thee. Blessed art thou amongst women and blessed is the fruit of thy womb, Jesus. Holy Mary, mother of God, pray for us sinners now and at the hour of death. Amen. On my knees, leaning against our bed, hands folded, I listen in silence. She is near, but overcome with fatigue, I lie down.

The top sheet flutters as if a warm breeze is above. She is Sublime. The massage loosens Fear, and he retreats, though I do not know where because I do not think about him. My mind and then my body fade into a deep rest.

As I attend Mass on holy days of obligation and observe Advent and Lent, I refer to the liturgical calendar in measuring time, and I raise our children within the four walls of the Church. They understand the protocols of Mass, if not its importance, and they learn at an early age to keep themselves tidy during the Liturgy; if they're not actively participating in it, they keep quiet and still, and I reward them for this.

"Mom, can we get two strawberry frosted so me and Sis can have one?"

"Yes, honey."

"I get it if there's only one left," her sister says.

"No!"

"I'm older."

"That's not fair."

"You have the vanilla frosted."

"Mom, tell Sis."

"Okay girls, that's enough. We just left Mass. You're supposed to love each other."

My girls' benign squabbling resonates with me, such is the pulse of life every Sunday for years, and in our home, I live, at least try to live, the words of The Little Flower, Saint Therese of Lisieux… the "little way" of "spiritual childhood," "doing the smallest right, and doing it all for love."

What does this mean for me? Everything. All my actions are intended as acts of love, an offering for my life to be a continuous prayer of thanksgiving like the Blessed Mother and Therese's. She was a fragile and diminutive nun whose unremarkable position in her convent eventually leads her to sainthood. I pick up her cross and serve my family through seemingly mundane chores. Each brings me closer to God and offers me the opportunity to bloom in love where I am planted.

All the furniture is back where it belongs, in my daughter's Barbie house. It is not clear what is happening, but it looks as though she decided it was better to stack it upstairs in the smallest room. After the beds are made and the chairs are tucked underneath the table, which is set for four, I shelve the household items. The convertible, packed with clothes, shoes and accessories, as though Barbie is relocating to another playhouse back east, is unpacked and everything is refolded and put in its storage bin. Accessories are organized too: shoes find their mates, as do socks, stockings, purses and hats. The convertible drives back to its parking place next to the house. Each Barbie's hair is brushed before being stored in another bin. My daughter's world revolves around her Barbies and her squeal of delight to find her passion organized and ready for her when she returns from school brightens my day.

All the lovely creatures from the Pet Shop and Pet Zoo are rounded up from the windowsills, the bookshelf, and family room. I return them to their carriers where they will reside until my older daughter releases them later in the day. She left books throughout the room, as well as unfinished puzzles. I put the puzzles together and restack them on the bookshelf. Then I collect the books and shelve them in alphabetical order according to subject or series. One of the Polly Pocket figures is missing, misplaced last evening somehow while the girls played. It is a nuisance because it is tiny, so tiny that I could have swept it up last night as the girls ran through the kitchen with arms full of stuff. Happily, it is underneath the base board heater in the dining room, and I return her to her case. When my eldest comes in after a swim in our pool, she will look for her figurines and will read her favorite books or complete a challenging puzzle, all the while singing out of key. Freshly baked cookies and milk will be placed next to her, and the way she bounces as she sits on the floor and eats fills me with joy.

My priority is devotion to his professional needs. I know his numbers: 16.5, 29, 3, 7 1/8, important numbers needed to keep his uniform tidy. It takes practice to press it correctly, and I learn early on if the creases are off by a minutia, dressing it is a challenge. Navy wings of gold are positioned above the left pocket, just above the crease, centered and straight. Above it ribbons are placed on their frame in descending order: most prestigious medals at the top, in his case, Meritorious Service, Navy Commendation and Navy Achievement medals. Any ribbon that shows a hint of wear is replaced. His collar insignia needs to be symmetrical as does the insignia on his piss cutter. He is particular, and on more than one occasion he fixes my errors, which motivate me to be better.

I make sure his meals are ready when he comes home from work. If he's late, he'll find it on the kitchen table covered with silverware and a napkin in their appropriate spots. He brings a beer in from the garage to have with the meal. I keep a record of his favorite dishes and rotate them throughout the month. Now and again I try new things, and if he likes them, I add them to the mix.

I take care of any errands. This can mean anything from going to the corner store for beer or the hardware store to picking up an item for him at the exchange. Whatever he needs me to do, I do in service to him and communion with The Little Flower.

I am a work in progress seeking that space, a plane that is not of this earth, but not quite heaven either. I struggle, for as much as I do, there is more I do not do. Is it silly to care about dusting and clean baseboards? I do not like to dust or scrub on my knees. Does it matter if the windows are streaked? Not crazy about window washing either. How about sheets and clothes without wrinkles? I can iron, my grandma made sure of that, but it is tedious and time consuming. I like to clean, cook, bake, and run endless errands for him to any number of places because I want his weekends to be free, but the "little way" requires love in all endeavors, so these lapses in my domestic responsibilities are impediments to spiritual growth. Still seeking, I dive deeper into the faith by adoring the Eucharist, taking time to open up to the power of The Christ, to divine energy, the fire of the Holy Spirit.

The lights in the sanctuary are low when we enter the church and take our seats in the first row of pews. Four white candles illuminate the altar, which is covered with a white altar cloth. The congregation hushes as Father comes into the sanctuary wearing a white alb and stole. A silk humeral veil is draped over his shoulders and down his front. It is white with golden threads running through it. He uses the veil to carry the monstrance, like we use potholders to carry a casserole to the dinner table. It contains the Eucharist: the body, blood, soul, and divinity of Christ, and as Father places it on the altar, he bows. Using the altar as a support, he kneels before the monstrance and prays. After he stands up, he picks up the censer, which looks like a medieval knight's armored helmet, stirs the incense in it, and once it is smoking, he swings it forward and backward on either side of the monstrance mouthing words the faithful cannot discern because his back faces us. He turns around, blesses us, and leaves in sacred silence when he is through.

I encourage the girls to kneel with me. We pray, "Saint Michael the archangel, defend us in battle. Be our protection against the wickedness and snares of the devil. May God rebuke him, we humbly pray, and do thou, O Prince of the Heavenly Host, by the power of God, cast into Hell Satan and all evil spirits who prowl about the earth seeking the ruin of souls." We make the sign of the cross, and the girls sit back in the pew.

They fidget. I lean over to them and promise to take them for a treat if they are patient. They slide across the slick wooden pew holding hands and giggle. "Shhhh," I say. Their eyes squinch and their shoulders laugh as they cover their mouths. My youngest takes hold of my dress and tugs it.

"I'll be right back. Don't worry, you are safe." I gently remove her hand, and her sister takes hold and draws her near.

In front of the monstrance, grasping for a prayer, I find none, but then a surge of energy flows into my body, through the soles of my feet, up my legs, into my core, to my head and out. It takes hold of me, golden and warm, and I watch it swirl before and around me. I am in the rapture: it is misty, but not wet, and I do not sense anything but an intense presence of something that must be divine love. I am at ease, and an overwhelming peaceful feeling, as though I am exactly where I am supposed to be, is joyful, but not fleeting as we often experience it in life. It is all consuming, yet unassuming. It is as though I am caught up in an energetic eddy, a vortex that connects me to the next world.

"Mommy, Mommy, let's go!" I hear the words faintly. "Mommy we want to go, please Mommy!" I do not respond. Side by side, the girls grab my dress, tugging, pulling me away, pulling and pulling until I cross the boundary between the supernatural and natural planes.

"Mommy, what's wrong?"

"Nothing's wrong, honey."

"Your face is shiny."

"Is it?"

Once I am able to calm them, the girls take hold of my dress again, each on either side of me, and we walk out of church. In the rapture, I live the essence of Love, the same essence I experienced in my bedroom the night before Daddy died.

I continue this path for many more years, until my son is sixteen and my girls are on their own. He announces he is no longer practicing the faith. "The leadership is terrible, full of hypocrites and do-nothings. I'm done with it." I do not blame him. The ongoing revelations about the sexual abuse scandals are shameful and a burden for the faithful to carry. I wish he could see beyond the institution, though, to the souls that make up its body and the wonder and beauty I experience. I say nothing. What fills the void is our Harley; and although I do not abandon my love for Christ, his blessed mother and the saints I am drawn to, I walk away from the Church too. I seek, with a sense of urgency, closeness to him, and look for us when we ride.

He buys it just before he retires from active duty and includes me in the process, which is a first, since he usually makes decisions about large expenditures himself. We decide the bike will be good for him and therefore, good for us. We give each other leather jackets and shop for accessories together.

"What are you doing?"

"I bought foot pads for you." He bends down while he adjusts it.

"Thank you." I kiss the top of his head.

"These are better than pegs."

"Oh?"

"Your foot won't slip, and I won't have to clean the sole of your boot off my pipes again."

"Can we go for a ride?"

"In a bit." He finishes his beer.

"Where are we going?" I straddle the Harley while he holds the bike steady.

With his skull on and moving his head up and down and then left to right, he secures it with the chin strap. He is not comfortable. "Damn helmet laws," he utters before he pulls out of the driveway.

It is a crisp fall day on the peninsula, sunny and in the mid-50s. We ride through Poquoson before easing onto 17, which runs through York County. As we pass old-time businesses like Winfree's Guns and Tobacco and Pop's Diner, I imagine what southern life on the peninsula was like back in the day: slower paced, deliberate and hospitable, certainly different than the hubbub of the northern cities and suburbs of my youth: congested environments one tries to keep pace with, certainly not environments one can manipulate.

Just before the Coleman Bridge, we exit onto Colonial Parkway, a twenty-three-mile scenic road linking the three points of Virginia's historic triangle: Jamestown, Williamsburg and Yorktown. It runs parallel to the York River.

The road invites him to release the Harley from the convention of the ride in town to a scenic thoroughfare, and even though it has limits and constraints, he opens her up. Our bodies meld: We submit to her rhythm as she transitions from gear to gear, leaning us backward then forward, until she purrs in overdrive.

He lifts his bottom off the seat slightly to unfurl his bunched jeans, and then he sinks low in his seat but keeps his back straight. He fiddles with his helmet, loosening the chin strap and then placing his open palm on top of it, he forces his head to submit to Virginia law again. His feet rest on the crash bar, and he scans from left to right before he turns up the radio and rides. I sidle up to him, spread my legs open enough to feel the swell of his back against my pelvis; and then, close my inner thighs against his hips, slightly flexed. My breasts rest against his backside and with my arms wrapped around his waist, I hold him. The smell of leather compels me to touch it.

As I squeeze, it oozes between my fingers while I rub my left cheek back and forth on his back. We ride through a pile of leaves; flashes of yellows and reds are before my eyes, and I close them as he opens the throttle on the straightaway.

He leans against the railing at the front of the ferry; the breeze sweeps across his face and through his hair as he looks down river. I want to know what he is thinking about. Where is he? Does the water lull his angst? Give him hope for us? Does he even think about us? I sit on the bike, bask in the sun, watch him and take note of his military stance and hair; finally free after years of service, it is long and he wears it in waves that compliment his face, which is weathered but still handsome after so much time at sea. His gray sideburns give him a distinguished air. *If only he were in touch… if only he would look at me as I look at him.*

"I thought we'd go to Bacon's Castle." He turns to me as I approach. "It's about five miles into Surrey."

"Interesting name." I lean over the railing and look down at the water. The river is beautiful, it goes on and on.

"I think the name comes from Bacon's rebellion."

"Oh?"

"It was occupied by a dude named Bacon during the 1600s uprising."

"I hope it has a garden."

We ride Route 10, the backroads of the peninsula, past cotton fields, tobacco fields, and peanut farms, through Smithfield, Rescue and Battery Park, astride our hog as she negotiates Nike Park Road, first leaning us left into the S turn and then right on the other side. I surrender to the ride, and like a trip on a magic carpet ride, there is much to behold that invigorates my senses.

When I was in college, I read *Zen and the Art of Motorcycle Maintenance*, a story about a man on a journey within a journey, reflecting on his troubled mind, seeking to discern sanity, if possible, while riding cross country on his vintage motorcycle making repairs along the way. It is a story of the moment and what it brings with the ride, be it a blown spark plug or insight. My rides with him animate the themes of the story, giving me insight not only into the biking experience but also myself.

There are not any inhibitions on the road. It welcomes all to experience the world without an agenda. The ride is Zen, liberation from time, an opportunity to experience the moment, to live it unconcerned with the past and future: to accept the invitation to a meditative practice of surrendering to the eternal now. When I ride with him, I do not think about our years together, our accomplishments as parents and individuals, those times we connect, though they are few and in the distant past. We are squared away, and the vibrations created by the bike's transmission urge me to let go. I love the intimacy of the ride with him, and I cherish it because he is my captive on the road. The disagreements, the widening distance between us and the decline of our relationship do not exist in the eternal now. I ride with him, and I believe we can make it. How can I think differently in the moment?

The Boulder-Vanocker Loop is a two hour 40-mile excursion in the Black Hills. It takes us through golden canyons painted from sun rays and accented with wild grasses at the base of their crags, and creeks meander along with us babbling their greetings. One open meadow is saturated with goldenrod; it huddles within the confines of the trees and looks like nature's picnic blanket.

He shifts gears continuously because the curves are acute. My arms around his waist and my thighs squeezing his, I wrap myself around him, and we weave, leaning as we come into the curve and then leaning out to position ourselves for the next one. Together, we climb higher and higher, and we do not slow down; the Harley responds, giving him the power to manage the near-vertical slope as though we are riding an aircraft after take-off. I see the expanse of the hills as we crest, varying shades of green and rock blend together to create a pre-historic landscape; I believe beneath its surface lay creatures waiting to be uncovered. He downshifts as we decline, keeping her speed consistent and the ride smooth. Still weaving, I hold on and follow his lead until we reach the straightaway and Big Mama's Beer Garden, a popular watering hole for bikers: "If the gate is open, so are we!"

We ride to The Mangy Moose, an open-air bar that sits on Main Street in Hill City. It attracts artists and unique retailers, and I enjoy strolling through studios and clothing stores. One captures my attention because their dresses remind me of eighteenth-century western saloon garb sewn together with a dash of sixties bohemian.

One day I notice he has taken my seat off the Harley. No reason, just a shrug and a remark, "You don't like riding." I do not say anything, and I wait, but he rides alone, sometimes gone for several hours, and I do not ask where he has been. He joins a bike gang and finds companionship with them. Without our ride, I cannot seek him, and since we share our home with a menacing presence keeping us apart, we live alone. He sits in our family room in the dark drinking beer, watching TV and scrolling through Facebook. I choose to tune him out and tune in talk radio in the evenings, preferring the rancor of federalists to our acrimonious relationship. This is living and I continue to live like this after he is gone because it is all I know how to do.

I exist, but I come to define 'seeking' through my visits with Sharon; and it is clear it is my truth, not familial, marital or spiritual expectations I have lived with all my life. And so, I begin the journey to it, and I start with yoga.

It becomes part of my daily routine. I learn how to breathe purposefully and meditate. Through Vinyasa and Hatha practice, I become aware of my body's language, visualizing my energy system moving unobstructed through it facilitates physical healing. My body responds well to yoga, sopping it up like Italian bread in marinara sauce.

I make a pilgrimage to Esalen Institute in Big Sur, California to attend a five-day yoga retreat. Embracing the opportunity, I decide all I need to do is show up, so I fly to San Francisco and then catch a shuttle to the institute.

He and I lived in Monterey, California. The climate is ideal: always sweater weather, and Big Sur is about twenty-three miles south. As the shuttle passes through it, I reminisce about a brief, promising time in my marriage. He and I are in our late twenties with two children and a dog.

"What are those?" my daughter asks.

"Peacocks," he says. "Look at that one, it's spreading its feathers."

"Are those eyes?" She stops.

"No, those aren't eyes."

"What are they?"

"Designs, maybe they help peacocks know who is who."

"Is it a girl?"

He bends down. "It's a boy, and boy peacocks are prettier than girl peacocks." He glances up at me and gives me that boyish look, the one I cannot resist.

As the shuttle passes by the Monterey exit, I press my left hand against the glass window. *I never imagined I'd be here like this.* I close my eyes once it is out of sight and try to nap.

Esalen is described as "heaven on earth", and I am inclined to agree. Perched atop a cliff overlooking the Pacific Ocean, it exists as one hundred and twenty acres of fertile soil once nurtured and cultivated by the Esselen people five thousand years ago. Farmers and naturalists embrace Esalen's mission, a mission dedicated to human transformation through body, mind, heart and spirit integration, a mission in tune with the natural world.

My eyes find the flower garden off to the right as the shuttle pulls in. Yellows, whites, pinks, and blues mingle atop the cliff, as though they are posing for Monet, bathing in the sunlight; though obscured, it warms the flower heads whose stems are thick. Nothing languishes there, and I surmise the loam is especially fertile given its history and the care it receives.

The commanding surf edges up against the rocky coast rhythmically, and my ears pick up on it and lead my body to the edge of the cliff. Leaning on the railing, I look over it, bent at the waist and inhale the salt sea air with my eyes closed. I look left and then right, back and forth several times slowly, after I open them, experiencing the beauty of the grasses, succulents and native flowers that blanket the base of the cliffs in reds, yellows, and shades of green. Above them, reaching high in the sky and into the mist are the rocky formations that epitomize the west coast- majestic, ancient, and formidable. At Esalen the ocean reaches out to the mountains, and the mountains reach back. They blend into each other seamlessly, creating an exquisite coastline... fantastic, and though out of reach, it is tangible, like a concept whose time has come.

I collect my belongings, a small suitcase and my yoga mat, at the front office and go to my room, which is quite small, after I check in. I share this space with three other women: two Europeans and one native Californian. *This is perfect, I will want for nothing.* I put my things away in the closet, exchange "hellos" with my roommates, and go back outside. *You only have five days... no time to unpack.*

I gravitate to the lodge, a spacious gathering space for meals and fellowship. The Lodge is similar to the dining hall in the movie *Parent Trap*, wooden tables with benches, high vaulted ceilings with a homey feel. It is warm with an endless supply of coffee, tea and toast. It accommodates seekers, intellectuals and hippies, not pre-adolescent campers dressed in uniforms.

I take a seat amid all the activity after I get a cup of tea. One of my roommates comes in, and I watch her pour herself a cup of coffee. Our glances meet.

"I'm Bridget." She extends her hand.

We greet each other as women do. "Where do you live in Germany?"

"The city of Berlin."

"Is your family from East Berlin?"

"We are from West Berlin." She smiles. "You come from?"

"Virginia." She raises her eyebrows. "On the east coast of America, close to Washington D.C."

"Ah, I see, yes. What do you do?"

"I teach."

"Me too!"

"What do you teach?"

"English, do you teach English also?"

"I enjoy writing instruction, and I do a lot of that. I'm also a special education teacher."

"Ah, yes, I see." She sips her drink. "Is this your first visit to Esalen?"

"Yes, and it's more than I hoped for: the gardens, the water, all of it."

"Ah, yes, me too."

"Is this your first visit to America?"

"Yes, I travel through Europe, now here."

"I want to go there someday."

"What are you doing here?"

"I'm here to practice yoga and meditation."

"Me also, but I changed to uh… leadership program because I'm not serious with yoga. I don't care what I do, I just want to be here."

"I get it." I stir my tea slowly and look out the window to the horizon.

She moves next to me. "Are you good?"

"I hope so. My eyes scan the tabletop. I just got divorced after a long marriage. I'm still finding my way."

Bridget's eyes fill with tears. "I loved too… nine months ago it ended." She wipes her eyes.

I touch her hand. "I'm sorry."

Our eyes smile, and we squeeze our hands together.

Big Sur is currently fighting a devastating forest fire in Pfeiffer State Park. Ash drifts down to us daily, and the winds blow smoke into our community, sometimes blocking the sunshine; however, in the evenings when the sun begins its descent, that same overcast creates a vision. The sun glows deep red, as if Zeus, while sitting on his throne at Mt. Olympus, extends his arm down to the vegetable garden and picks the most perfectly round and reddest tomato and places it in the sky. What a wonder it is, a wonder I have the privilege to experience every evening because two careless people didn't bother to respect the natural world's limitations during the dry season.

Other yogis gather in the yurt. Once we are assembled, our teacher, Pia, asks us to sit in a circle. We number forty-five... forty-five seekers, each with a different story to share. Many people are blissful, content in life, desiring to grow in their practice. Some are battling cancer, others are in recovery, and some are on their own, like me, after years of marriage. *I'm here to find the woman I forgot about and hopefully, understand.* It feels good to be brave, and the positive energy circling above us is discernable. When we join hands, it passes through us. Pia says, "Let's bring our hands to heart center. The light in me honors the light in you. Namaste." She bows, and we do too.

We immerse ourselves in Kundalini, integrating breathing techniques, movement, chanting and meditation, while building physical stamina and consciousness. Pia also incorporates Vinyasa practice into our routine. She tells us, "I will show you a high better than anything you can get out there." She does! I am alert, fully present; in fact, I am high all day long, even experiencing euphoria at times. In bed by midnight and up by 4 a.m. every morning, I shower and then soak in the hot springs tub while I watch the sun rise. *Everything is clear here: who I can be, who I want to be.*

"Be aware of what your body is doing," Pia instructs us. "What is it telling you?" I sit crossed legged, my lower back propped up with a Mexican blanket, my arms resting on my thighs, my wrists on my knees, the tips of my thumbs and pointer fingers touch making first mudra: individual and universal awareness. I experience a sensation, the movement of energy through my body, starting at my root chakra and working its way up toward my crown. Pia leads us. "Take a deep breath through your nose using three-part breathing. Expand your abdomen with the inhale, feel the breath as it fills your lungs, inhale, deeper to a count of seven, keep holding, tighten your root, your sacral, tighten everything… hold it… *Sat*. Now exhale, release your breath to the count of seven, feel it empty from your lungs, to your abdomen, completely exhale until your navel contracts into your core… *Nam*. Feel the energy within pulsating and circulating. Be still and in the moment, know your body," she says. *Sat Nam*: truth is my identity. I chant these words and incorporate them into my lexicon. *Sat Nam*: truth is who I am.

Pia sits up straight, smiles and begins. "Be comfortable. We are going to practice breath of fire for nine minutes." The sole of my right foot is against my root chakra, the sole of my left foot is against the shin of my right leg. She chimes in, "We will place our arms in first mudra for three minutes, extend them out to the sides for the next three minutes, palms up, and the final three minutes our hands will be at heart center." She demonstrates: "Put the palms of your hands together, left thumb over right if you are a woman, the other way if you are a man." Her soulful smile radiates. "Interlock your fingers so the pinky of the right hand is on the outside," She holds her hands up.

"Extend your pointers to the heavens." She then places her thumbs between her breast plates. "Breath of fire is short exhales through the nose quickly, like this." Pia breathes rapidly and loudly, in short bursts. "We have tissues if you need them." She sets her timer and we begin. Breath of fire elevates my mind and spirit. It stimulates my solar plexus, generating heat and releasing energy throughout my body, something I need to do to journey within. In what seems like no time, I am floating.

Pia says, "Feel the energy in your body, be in this moment, clear your head." My body is still and relaxed. My arms rest on my thighs, my hands are wrapped around my knees. I am awake, but I am not in the yurt. At some point my left arm slips off my thigh and falls to the floor. The thud echoes. "Mmmm," is Pia's response.

"Find yourself someplace…" I am in a forest filled with tall trees, pines, and scrub oaks. There is water, a large lake, sparkling, dappled sunlight illuminates the forest floor. Pia says, "See the temple there before you go to it." It is in a large clearing surrounded by trees, and it looks like it is created for the temple. Bathed in light, it glistens white with three huge Roman columns and countless marble steps. Though intimidating, I climb them without a struggle.

"Who is there?" Pia asks. Daddy. He greets me, smiling and holding his arms out to me. "Open the temple doors... who is there?" Christ as I remember him from childhood. The three of us share the moment silently. His Transfiguration comes to mind, though Moses and Elijah aren't with Him. Alice, the yogi to my right, walks through my vision, which begins to fade as Pia brings us back. During supper, we share our experiences late into the night.

Leaving Esalen is difficult because its positive vibe is potent. I am awake there; drawn into its breath and heartbeat and able to connect to experiences beyond self. I am Zen. The people and I are like-minded, and we are close in our moments together, but we do not know if we will come back, though we want to, and yet, we accept what is and do not concern ourselves with what could be. Although I return home with a stronger sense of self, my truth eludes me; and within a year, I desire more, and another path is laid before me. It is up the James river as far as Buckingham county, among the Virginia mountains splashed with reds and yellows. It is an ashram.

Satchidananda Ashram is the headquarters of Swami Satchidananda's documented teachings. His goal is interfaith understanding as a vehicle to world peace. His Lotus temple is a testament to his willingness to embrace all faiths, even faiths yet unknown... *There are many paths to the one truth.* This is the lesson at the ashram, and the peacefulness that circulates around it quiets my spirit, even the cold mountain air is tolerable, and I walk freely throughout campus without a sweater all weekend. I wake each morning before sunrise to practice and meditate with advanced souls, and it is during these times I release the chatter in my mind. Unlike the kundalini practice, I do not arouse my energy. I sit with it while I am led to my peaceful inner self. It is here I feel my calling; it is here I embrace it when these words are shared by our group leader just as I come out of my meditative state Sunday morning, "You are a divine being having a human experience." *I am a divine being having a human experience. I am a divine being having a human experience… nine words… nine life changing words… the nine words I am ready to hear and ingest. This is my truth. Sat Nam.*

16
Healing

*W*hat are you grateful for? I glance at my reflection in the bathroom mirror before I turn away. "I am grateful for my children, health, work…" *This is not that question,* a voice says, *the hackneyed one everyone asks with the prescribed answer.* I know. This is *the* question, and it comes from the depths to the surface as a fish does when it feeds. Its answers are sustenance; they are what binds me to myself and grounds me to Earth.

I do not have answers, at least this is what I tell myself. Lying on my bed late in the night and staring at the ceiling, I do know some things, though. I am weak, even though I have been in counseling for nearly two years. I cling to Fear; his power is intoxicating at times, and after I sober up from an encounter with him, I am hung over, spent; I resolve to release him and break the addiction, but I cannot. Anger is still close by too. And him? He is still with me, apparently another addiction I need to wrestle with. I toss and turn until early morning and I get up before the sun. It is always this way the night before I see Sharon.

"I can't let him go, can I? I still cling to his words and actions." I pause. "I want control and I don't see it as a bad thing; I see it as something I need."

"You can't control what has been. You can control the choices you make moving forward and you can construct your reality, but do you think any of us has any genuine control?"

"I don't know Sharon. I don't want to fall into the same patterns again."

"Awareness of where you've been will keep you from doing that."

Silence.

"Was I ever good enough for him?"

"I think you know the answer."

"I felt his presence all around me, even when he was at sea. I saw him looking over my shoulder whenever I planned, decided, or spent money. His influence was transcendent. How did he do this?"

"He didn't do anything."

"What?"

"You allowed this. You allowed him to watch over you. You allowed him to influence you. You reacted, you didn't respond."

"Why? Why did I allow him?"

"You surrendered your power to him."

"But why? Why would I do this?"

"You need to come to understand why."

"How am I supposed to do this?"

"Think of yourself as crystal."

Silence.

"A crystal has many angles, grooves and edges, some flat, some beveled. It's nearly impossible to see what encompasses the entirety of crystal. It's something you look at from many perspectives."

"I am a crystal?"

"You're multi-dimensional. You're going to need to look at yourself from many perspectives. It takes time to come fully into ourselves, but if you're willing to look again and again, you can get there."

"There?"

"Oneness with the Creator."

"In this life?"

"Perhaps."

"This is a lot, Sharon."

"It is."

"I feel I need to understand what happened in my marriage before I can begin to grasp the eternal."

"You allowed yourself to react to him. This was your pattern of behavior."

Silence.

"You observed his behavior toward you and then you conducted yourself accordingly. I think you still allow him to look over your shoulder."

Silence.

"You're your own woman." Sharon pauses, "Remember when people were asking 'what would Jesus do?'"

"Yes."

"You did this with him… What would he do? No more of this."

Silence.

"Were you good enough for your mother?"

"Who knows?"

"I think you do."

"I did what was expected of me."

"When did this begin?"

"I was a girl."

"Did you measure up?"

"No, I couldn't measure up to her."

"How did you know?"

"She'd tell me and then I felt guilt for not being what she needed, so I kept trying."

"And did you?"

"What?"

"Do what she wanted?"

"I suppose, but it was hard to know what to do. I didn't want to hear her complaints anymore. I was her daughter, not a confidant."

"Your mother was happy with him?"

"Yes. Being with him pleased her, and it felt good to live without guilt. I fell in love with him, at least what I thought falling in love was, and it was nice that my mother supported this."

"You were good together in some respects."

"We were both responsible and doers. We knew how to conduct the business of marriage, and we knew what parenting meant."

"You were a match, so you married."

"We did fit, at least I thought so."

"And?"

"I tried to do what I was supposed to: be submissive and deferential, raise the children, and manage the house."

"Your mother and he had expectations, and so did you, but you chose to follow others' expectations, not your own."

Silence.

"Why didn't you have faith in yourself?"

"I've made some poor choices."

"What does this mean?"

Silence.

"You learned from those choices?"

"I had an abortion when I was nineteen."

Silence.

"I told him about it, and I went to a priest for forgiveness."

"Have you forgiven yourself?"

Silence.

"Have you?"

"I don't know. I'm haunted at times… and angry, and he used it to hurt me."

"He didn't do anything."

"It's Fear, isn't it? Fear keeps me on the defensive."

"And Anger?"

"Anger blocks energy and keeps me from growing."

"And forgiveness too. At the heart of all of this is your willingness to forgive yourself."

"For the abortion?"

"For everything, anything."

Silence.

"Your mission is to know who you are and love her."

"What does that mean?"

"Accept what is and who you are in this moment. She is enough. I promise."

Silence.

"You have a decision to make going forward. You've lived the obligatory pattern, now you can choose to live the choice pattern, making decisions based on your expectations, no one else's, knowing you have learned along the way."

Sharon takes notes. "How long have you lived with Fear?"

"Since Daddy died."

"Why did you let him in?"

"If God can take your father, anything is possible."

"You can't think this?"

"I was a little girl, and his death took a piece of me. What was I supposed to do? They told me it was God's will."

"Anger and resentment?"

"They showed up in my teens."

"Why hang onto Fear?"

"He's like an old shoe."

"And the others?"

"They let me know what I feel is appropriate, that what happened is not my fault."

"What happened is no one's fault."

Silence.

"Are you prepared to live with this? You can convince yourself that it's your right to be angry and resent him because of the way he treated you, but is this how you grow into your higher self?"

"I don't care sometimes."

"We've talked about victimhood."

"This isn't that. He made choices too!"

"He did, and many of them were poor choices you had to live with, but you need to let them go."

"How can I expect to live a lifetime without these emotions? They are part of the human condition."

"They are, but you want to connect to the divine, and to do that, you must recognize what these human emotions do."

"What do they do?"

"They block energy. They keep you unbalanced. They can cause physical illness. They keep you from living your higher self."

"I can only hope to be a saint."

"We are called to be saints. Our goal is Oneness, ascension to life. Part of that experience is recognizing our condition and then transcending it."

"To?"

"To the realization that we are infinite awareness; we are all connected, and we need to wake up, to live from the heart with love. We all come from God who is love."

"To forgive and understand, right?"

"Yes, and to be grateful for life, for any circumstance that comes your way, faithful that what comes to you, ultimately teaches, sustains, brings and keeps you connected to the divine."

"I know similar lessons."

"There is injustice in the world and extreme inequality too, and when we can we reach out and help."

"But—"

"But I keep myself bathed in the light. I understand what happens on this plane happens. My focus is on the light, oneness with The Creator."

"I like to think of myself as a woman who lives in the light, but maybe I don't anymore, maybe I never have; maybe, I thought I did because I was a faithful Catholic."

"Living in the light is not fixed, one grows in it."

"Not me, not in the last few years."

"Stop."

"I'm sorry.

"Don't be… know you are."

Silence.

"It will be a challenge to choose love, and there will be an internal struggle between the light and humanity, but the light is always stronger, certainly strong enough to blind you to Fear, Anger and Resentment."

"My light is buried under a bush, Sharon."

"You're blocked."

"How?"

"You'll find your way. Focus on the positive coming into your life. Let go of the negative. It does nothing for you."

"I'm still trying to be grateful."

"Let's go to the table and see what your body says."

I see her, but only in silhouette. She is mist in a woman's form. She hears the flute, its haunting melody spirals around her figure and she moves to it. She drifts toward me as she loses shape. Another melody wanders in and she expands in another direction until there is no form, just mist; and in it, I see life; it is a prism. A tear falls for as long as the note is held. Another tear falls with the next note and then again and again. It is serene, and I drift off.

"Your third eye is open," Sharon says.

"I think I'm beginning to understand."

"Oh?"

"It came to me."

"That makes sense."

"Why?"

"I saw the shackles."

"You did?"

"Yes... I took them off."

It is early evening and I wander the garden. She is getting ready for rest. Leaves nestle at the base of trees and are ready to insulate them when the cold arrives. The butterfly garden is stripped of its food. The milkweed and fennel are a collection of barren stems, an eyesore to the casual observer but a testament of a productive season to the mindful gardener. I have a few blooms: toad lily, *Camelias*, native *Echinacea* and *Helianthus*. I crouch down by one of the water gardens and clear the debris carefully so I do not disturb the leopard frogs that hibernate at the bottom. I am amazed and saddened simultaneously; they are welcome neighbors who chose my garden; and though it is their time to take refuge before the ravages of winter, I will miss them jumping amongst the cardinal flower and *Rudbeckia* or sunbathing on daylily leaves. Oh! Above my head, a magnificent spider's web extends from the gutter to the eave! How I love the spiders who take up residence throughout the beds in fall! My affinity toward them is equal to my affection for butterflies. The former is my totem, the latter my spirit animal.

"I am grateful for you," I say to the garden, "I am sorry you are a mess, but even so, you make me happy. Thank you for your gifts this season." It is a start, somewhat propitious, so I take my cue from the spider, who represents power, growth and the shadow side and the butterfly, the symbol of transformation, and I sit on the porch chair to face the proverbial music.

Earlier, in a dark moment, I went to a dealership. My romantic self wants to write that my journey there was a lark, but it was not; it was a desperate attempt to recapture what I perceive as lost. It was our place, though we split soon after we begin riding, it is somewhere we go together, and being together is rare and even rarer is being together sharing an interest; and this happens at this particular dealership.

I convince myself I want to ride like I had with him. The ride with him is Zen and I want that feeling back. I enroll in a weekend course designed to give me the skill I need and the credential to do it. As I struggle to shift gears smoothly, I stall, and trying to maintain the appropriate speed while shifting is not pretty; and I doubt my ability and coordination. I understand riding a moped is nothing like riding a motorcycle. I persevere and make it through day one with my limbs and faculties intact, but I am rattled. I think this process should be easy, but I am not sure anymore, and I do not know if I will make it through. Knowing Zen is at stake, I wake up early on Sunday, review the ride in my mind and will myself to get through the day, which I do impressively while I maneuver through an obstacle course, an exercise of acceleration and deceleration, and negotiate an acute curve with the bike tires straddling the arc on a line.

I go back to the Harley dealer and promptly buy a bike. I am beaming at it sitting in my driveway one week later. After I change my clothes, I hop on and ride, first around the neighborhood, then out into the world, and what I think will usher in Zen turns out to be a disaster, and I know this because my body screams, "What are you thinking!" It shakes while I ride. Zen? It is there on the road, but I cannot find it because I need to focus on riding. Though disappointed, the lesson is learned, and a new home is found for the bike.

Finally, it is time to face what took me more than two years to confront. I am co-dependent, and as such, would rather think of myself as a bit of a martyr, a woman who "stands by her man" through his emotional sandstorm.

"Know your place," he says, and I comply because I feel for him. I know the stories he shares in moments of doubt. I am there! "I'm sorry you felt this way… I'm sorry no one saw what your dog meant to you… It was cruel for it to be taken away one day while you were at school… here, I'll get you a beer and I'll get supper started." There are other stories, the guitar under the bed that should have been his but was given to the eldest, and the Easter basket hidden in a place no five-year-old would look. They laugh at you as you run around the house in a panic. Yes, I see it all underneath the surface: the hurt, anger and shame. Sharon is right, we were a match!

Lost in our issues, we flounder together. For me, life is good if I do not have to deal with negative emotions that terrify me and transport me to sad places and arouse feelings of guilt and shame. It is much easier for me to please, please, please as often and as much as I can. You treat me as if I am gum on the bottom of your shoes: gooey, annoying, hard to shake, but I stick to you despite your efforts and choose to pity you, to reason that your demanding and outrageous behavior toward me comes from your past. I must accept it. If I do not, I must navigate through an emotional labyrinth of my own, and Fear keeps me from doing this. It is better to buffer, be subservient and neurotic. No wonder my sister calls me the "Show Pony," while my sister-in-law thinks I may need help because I am constantly cleaning and washing. I do not see what they see; I see a woman who loves her husband and wants him happy.

But you are never happy. There is never enough money, time, or people in your life who know how to think. Your arrogance is not endearing, but I pacify you anyway and live with your attitudes, ones that extend to me, and yet, I think you love me. You are a bit damaged, and I get it, and I love you through it because I am hopeful we will be all right in the end. I get increasingly angry with you, but I hide it from the children as best I can and perhaps, you as well; Anger's closest ally is Resentment, and he joins me since both travel in tandem. Together, they engage me in a game of tug of war, and I am no match for them, but I try anyway, and I tire, so I give up and give in until I cannot look at myself in the mirror. I blame you for all our troubles, but there is no blame, not really. I am the rich soil in which the seeds of mutual dysfunction are planted. I tend the garden and you water it, but the harvest is sparse and there is no fruit on the vine. The one exception is the children. We are intelligent, and we know we have "stuff" going on. We also know our issues were brought into the marriage in suitcases we tossed in the closet and never unpacked, and without exchanging words, we agree we will do better for our children, and we do, but their sense of selves I attribute to the intercession of The Blessed Mother rather than our parenting skills.

I think a lot about the meaning of love, and it frightens me that I may have not loved you. I have affection for you still, and I hope we can learn to be together with our children. You find a woman you say truly loves you and does not annoy or irritate you, and I make a grandiose statement about having to work hard for retirement because you said you are no longer able to work. Is my sacrifice of guaranteed income security evidence of true love?

In my devotion to Saint Teresa, love supposedly motivates me to serve my family with earnestness. Anger and Resentment are not there with me, at least not as far as our children are concerned. It is a hectic time in life when we are raising them, and as I write this, I see us doing what needs to be done without a connection; yet, oddly enough, we are connected. I have a vision while Sharon works on me, and I see the cord of light that keeps us connected, and as you walk away it stretches, and I see now the abyss between us. How sad, how very sad. Co-dependents do not love; they feed off each other. This is the most difficult to grasp, but the most important as well. It feels like love; it hurts like love; it presents itself as love, but it is not healthy, and it cannot endure. It sustains us for thirty years, through twenty-six years of service, three children, dogs and cats. The end.

Perhaps I need to give Love a break. I put tremendous pressure on this four-letter word. Why do I need to hear it said to me? Are my expectations for a fulfilling life dependent on the ability to bring about the proclamation, "I love you" or others to define the word for me? Throughout childhood, adolescence, and adulthood love has eluded me, except for a very brief moment when I know it well through one person, Daddy: He loves his tomboy, her wild hair, dirty knees and rebellious nature. We connect, and there is no need to mention the feeling's name; it needs no introduction. But this was many lifetimes ago, and though I cannot forget this man, the best man of my life, the one who shares love with me, I need to reacquaint myself with it, but this time through my eyes only. I need to take a long, hard look in the mirror.

17

Homecoming

I hear a wren at the empty feeders for the first time in over two years, even though it is there daily throughout the season literally, I presume, singing for its supper. I listen to its lovely song while I lean on the deck railing remembering the mornings spent in the garden weeding, planting, and daydreaming about him, us, our life once the children are grown and the beautiful garden I would create for it.

He shows me a picture of a hedge of daylilies from one of my books. "These. I like these."

"Those are daylilies."

"Whatever. Can you plant those?"

This is music to my ears, and I plant a small bed out front with a variety of cultivars with warm colors. Daffodils keep them company and the two coexist marvelously: the former's greenery, which cannot be cut back after its flower is spent, is hidden by the greens of the daylilies as they come into season. He sees them each time he pulls into the driveway, and I make the effort to keep the spent daylily flowers out of the bed. I pull any dead leaves to generate new growth; though my lilies only bloom once, the luscious chartreuse green leaves add texture and interest to the bed. I never take to the Stella D'oro variety that blooms throughout the season. Their flowers are not spectacular, and the quality of subsequent blooms diminishes as the season progresses. One year he plants just about a flat of impatiens, which both surprises and pleases me.

"Don't get too excited, Woman," he tells me as he hands me eight plants from the flat. "Here, you can have these." I plant them in the bed with cardinal flower and much to my delight they thrive the next several years, spreading themselves out along the entire bed until a blight comes through the region and kills them. What a sad time for all gardeners who enjoy this annual that gives with all its might throughout the season. He plants mums for a few seasons. Autumn is his favorite time of the year as far as I can tell: football, pumpkins, Thanksgiving and mums. Not my favorite, I want to him to reconsider the mums, but he is adamant and tells me not to touch them or the bed they live in. It is difficult for me to resist pruning them at the end of the season, and one year I do prune them because I cannot tolerate their spindly stems. I get an earful about it, but honestly, it is worth the tongue lashing.

I rip them out the day after he leaves and claim the bed. The empty bed reminds me of what once was and will never be and it needs to be planted, but for the life of me, nothing comes to mind. It is as though it needs to stay as it is, and I cannot avoid it because it is the one piece of the garden that is barren.

As a girl I spent hours in my head escaping this world for any number of reasons, most of all sadness and loneliness, but these emotions are not with me today. I am better off on my own, content with solitude; it fortifies me, and still grappling with shame and guilt, it is a necessity.

You should have tried harder, maybe you should have learned to live with him, not as you wanted, but as it was. You had the children and grandchildren to consider too. Nagging thoughts like these still ring in my ears. Reason offers his thoughts. *Your husband stays, even though he stops meeting your needs, to make sure your children grow up with their father. This is good. Now he is home after serving his country for almost thirty years. This is also good, he earns this; and his choice to be there without you is his choice.* I hold on to this thought, embrace it, but it wriggles in my arms and I drop it. Reason's influence cannot match Anger who picks up the thought and throws it at me. *Shit!* He casts me as a victim again, and I capitulate. *How could you give up after so many years? I stood by you, loving you through it all!* I dance in a circle. *How could you allow yourself to be in this position? Maybe if you had said something earlier, things could have been different. You allowed him to shit on you.* Anger turns me around and around until I am sick to my stomach. I sit at the top of the deck's stairs.

As I face the patio he installed, I think about all the evenings he chose to lounge there on his own. I think about the times I reached out to him.

"What are you doing?"

"What's it to you?"

"I'm interested."

"Whatever, Woman."

"Don't you think we should talk, maybe do something. Maybe I can plant something with the mums."

"Leave them alone! You have enough of the yard as it is."

"I know you like what I do. I saw you take pictures of the bog garden."

Silence.

"It is pretty and I'm glad you think so too." I go to him.

"What are you doing?"

"Let me sit with you."

"Are you through?"

"What?"

"Go."

Did I miss something? What could I have done to make it better for both of us? I just sit there and although the wren's song is agreeable, it unsettles me to the point where I cannot stand to listen to it. My body is on edge and I rise quickly and go inside.

I pace back and forth, up and down from the kitchen to the back room, around the dining room several times, even upstairs and downstairs before I resolve to do something. In the dining room in front of the credenza, I stop. Above it, a large, rectangular mirror hangs on the wall.

I see the reflection. She is familiar, but she is a stranger, too. Her hair is longer, grayer, and shiny. Her skin is the soft brown color it always is, and it is clean, clear, and firmer. In fact, I see a healthier woman, a woman who is committed to self. *When did the crows' feet perch there?* Smiling, I massage them with my finger while I consider her large, bright green eyes. She is me and we are friends, after all. I put both hands on the credenza as I lean in. It is time for us to visit.

He's moved on and so have the children. It's okay, we're okay because people move on. We know how to work through fear... no more guilt and shame. You know who you were in marriage and you know how you lived. Hold your head up and see the fruits of you work: three children who love you, and him. They take care of themselves and each other. No mother can ask for more than this. They want you happy! Let's choose to be happy. More than two years is enough time. Look what we have done... we looked within, we dug deep, and we retrieved what we lost. We're not done, though, and you know what I mean. I stand up and back away.

I stand in front of the sink and look out the window at my cats, who stand watch over the back garden. They are sweet boys. They are gifts from the universe: small, innocent gifts given to me to love and nurture after their traumatic beginning. Their mother is killed, and they lose a brother and sister before they are rescued from a shed on Forest Road. Their vulnerable faces are posted on Facebook and I happen to see them, and in an instant, I know they are mine, and I call their foster mother to let her know. I go to the rescue compound each Saturday morning to be with them as they recover from their ordeal until one day they leave with me and together, we share a new beginning, one I promise them will be safe. At first they are timid, but they now own the backyard and all who dare to enter it. My redhead, Jefferson, is more aggressive than his brother Adams, who I worry about out there on his own. I know Jefferson is strong; he went on a three-day walkabout when he was six months old. I feared the worst and was about to give up hope, after spending those days putting up fliers, alerting neighbors, and posting his face on social media, when he stumbled back into the garden tired and hungry but no worse for the wear. Adams, on the other hand, is assaulted early on by one of the feral in the neighborhood. The poor boy has puncture wounds on his thigh and stays indoors for a couple of weeks before braving the garden again.

You are strong, intelligent, with many years ahead of you. She is speaking to me: *I am coming.* Back at the mirror I say, *Will you face it with me? Yes. We are worthy, we have something to say… we won't let anyone take our truth! You're right… we need to stand up! There you go, now straighten up, shoulders back, eye on the prize. Prize? Yes,* I say, *prize. You know what it is… recognize it and claim it.*

My conversations with Sharon and experiences since the breakup have led to this. My third eye is open, the shackles are gone and the opportunity to do something is right here, in the eternal now. *I love you,* I whisper. Shifting, my energy begins to move. Anger retreats, I see light and seize it.

"Is there something around the house you can use? Hammer nails into wood? Old dishes?" Sharon said during a session as we discussed Anger and its destructive nature. "You need to release it." She was right, and I choose to confront this menace.

In the garage is a box of finishing nails and an old hammer, and out back on the deck lays a 2x6 walnut board. I pause to imagine myself hammering nails into it with enough force to purge anger, but then I remember walnut is very hard, and I do not have the strength to break it. *There must be something.* I lean against the island in the kitchen. My eyes focus on the ceramic flooring. *You enjoyed the challenge of that project, spending days measuring, cutting and laying tile, and you were quite pleased with your efforts. I was too.* Smashing the extra tiles is not a good idea, since one from the floor may need to be replaced.

Years of relocating across the country taught me less is more, and I am in the habit of having just what I need. I like the idea of throwing dishes, but I do not have any I can spare. There is Mother's fine china, which is completely out of the question, and there is my everyday ware given to me by my mother-in-law. It was her mother's good china and she used it for years but never liked the pattern. She gave it to me after she moved to Rapid City since my set, which was very inexpensive, was faded and worn. *Hmmm. Could I? What will she think? She didn't ask for the set when we separated, only a Christmas decoration she made years ago. The dishes have value; antique stores sell this pattern now, and you have originals. The hell with it! I'm not letting money get mixed up in this. Should I do this?* My still quiet voice speaks up. "Yes." They are in the cabinet to the left of the sink, and I move with little thought except to rid myself of Anger's grip.

The dishes are stacked evenly on three steps leading to the garage while I back my car out and then close the door. I must admit it is a bit exciting to take control and do something. Admittedly, my actions are unorthodox and for some shocking, I am sure, but I will not allow myself to consider any ramifications of the actions I am about to take. I am my own woman, and I accept responsibility for this behavior without shame.

There he is on the stairs as he was over two years ago, unsteady yet cocky, with a slur in his voice. "I am your pinnacle. You'll never do better than me."

"How dare you?" Anger is present; he holds onto me with an iron grip. "How dare you speak to me like this! You should feel the shame and guilt but I shouldn't!"

The image becomes clearer as I near and when it is within reach, I wave my hand in front of it and dismiss it from my presence. Atop the stairs, I turn and face the empty space.

With a plate in hand, I pause and etch this picture in my head: alone and poised to release, to cleanse as though I am being baptized, but not with holy water, rather with the will of a turtle who digs her way out of her sand-filled nest and scurries to the ocean to survive. It is in her nature to do so as it is mine to survive in this world where light and dark are clearly demarcated but need to be integrated until gray is found and peace is made with it. There are no certainties moving forward except the knowledge that expectations and choices will be mine made from a position of emotional strength grounded in personal truth. How can I go wrong?

"Fuck this!" The plate shatters and shards fly across the space to all four corners. There is a letdown, a sense that maybe I am mistaken, but then the words begin to flow, and this is exactly right.

"You were wrong to treat me so badly!" Smash!

"I was right sometimes, and you were wrong!" Smash!

"Fuck you and your arrogance!" Smash, smash, smash! I pick up another and another and throw them with Anger. We have a sweet tempo, one after the other.

"Your success was mine too! You made it, but you needed me!" I cuss too, badly, like a sailor on leave in New Orleans during Fat Tuesday.

My last words, "You don't rate to be my lover and husband," refresh me. There they lay, forty plates in hundreds of pieces, and I am not sure how it feels. My hands shake and a chill runs through my body. I move down to the second stair and pick up a teacup.

"Shit!" I throw another and then another.

"I don't want this hurt! I don't want this pain! I don't want this Anger!" I throw them quickly, again and again. Midway through the pile I scream, "How dare you let him treat you poorly! You have value! How dare you let him take your truth from you! You let yourself go, something you never would have done before!" With the last demitasses cocked, I yell, "Stay in the light, wife! You're not needed here!" It explodes against the garage door like a homemade cherry bomb.

My body is speaking; I sit and listen. The chill is muffled by a wave of warmth; and though I chalk it up to physical exercise, it is more than exertion I notice. Peace is close; she is coming. What I feel is the harbinger of her, but I do not have a name for it. Every move is confident because it is right. I know Peace is there, waiting. I am on the right path, and each piece of china I throw brings me one step closer to her. Anger is not pleased and urges me to stay close to him.

On the third step he is there but weakened; his reticence apparent, I go within and loosen his grip anchored in my liver. "He's losing his mooring!" I hear these words as two figures appear from out of the shadows, old friends I have not seen in a while. As I reach for the anchor line so do they, and they motion me to back off while they pull it up slowly, carefully, making sure Anger does not drift. One announces, "Anchor aweigh!" I shift. Anger reacts, and I lose balance. "Keep the line straight and pull," the other says. I see him, after he is brought to light, a red creature, pointy ears and stout, a caricature of the devil without the pitchfork. He is impotent and skedaddles with his tail between his legs.

I toss what is left with my old friends Forgiveness and Gratitude.

"Thank you for our children. Thank you for supporting me while I raised them. Thank you for what you could give. You had your struggles, it's okay. I understand now… I had mine too. I gave you my best, and it will have to do. I'm not to blame. No one is."

Forgiveness and Gratitude are two lovely ladies, translucent and identical in appearance: long, curly blonde hair, blue eyes, covered in white silk dresses with high collars and long sleeves. We chuckle and then laugh, and they remain with me while I clean up the mess.

That evening on the porch with a cup of chamomile tea, I sit with my kitties. They take turns sitting on my lap and each receives the love they seek, gentle pats and long strokes across their backs. Their purrs please me, and I am pleased with myself too.

I order *Illuminata* by Marianne Williamson, and when it comes, I open the package hastily, take out the book and open it to the table of contents. I run my finger up and down the pages until I find it: divorce ceremony, page 277.

A proper divorce ceremony includes an officiant and the parties divorcing. I take from it what I need: simple words of farewell. Before I proceed, I cut a five-foot piece of cording from a spool and tie one end on the garage door doorknob and the other around my waist. I read, "I come before you, God, not in joy, but in acceptance. I bless you, husband, and release you. Please forgive me. I forgive you. Go in peace. You will remain in my heart." I use scissors to cut the rope that symbolizes the dissolution of our marriage and sacrament; although my action is a contradiction of the Church, it is what needs to be done.

Since the separation, I have not been back to Mass, and I spend months agonizing over this. I make a choice to walk away in a fit of anger and what I thought I would long for and eventually come back to has not happened. I cannot forsake what was my life for thirty years, and I do not want to. It was the reality I constructed and those who view it as immutable will perceive as they do. I know better now. Reality is mutable. I do miss the solemnity of Mass and its significance, but I know my love for Christ is beyond the walls of any church. I have received his body, blood, soul and divinity hundreds of times throughout my life; he dwells within. We dwell within together, both cut from the same cloth, both divine. And the Blessed Mother is here with me too. The epitome of feminine power, I still look to her for guidance, but I would like to offer my friendship and be a companion for her someday. I am appreciative for all the lessons the Church offers and I am grateful for the gifts it gives to those who seek meaning in this world. My body warms as I write these words. I know I am ready.

I envision him on our family room sofa, on the end next to the end table and table lamp. He sits crossed leg with his reading glasses perched on his nose. Resting on his lap is a novel; his right hand supports it while his left picks up a tall glass of sweet tea. It looks as though the glass is sweating and he moves it away from his clothing while he drinks. After, he puts the glass down and wipes his hand on his pants. He swallows a gulp while he continues to read. He is as he was before life had its way with us: his hair and goatee groomed, in his 501 jeans and pocket t-shirt. He wears the slippers I gave him for Christmas. He is comfortable and at ease, which is good, and I can approach him without fear. I watch him as I put the scissors away in the kitchen and place the *Illuminata* on the bookshelf in front of him to the right. I take a deep breath, hold for a count of ten, and then exhale through my mouth. I go to him, barefoot, in black yoga pants and a white kurta. I place my hand on his shoulder.

He says, "What have you done with your hair?"

"I grew it."

"What are you wearing?"

"I practice yoga in these clothes."

"Really?"

I smile. "Yes."

"For years you said you would."

"I wonder if I would, had we stayed together."

"Why am I here?" He closes his book, takes off his glasses and places both on the end table.

"I want my energy back," I say. "You can't have it anymore."

"Are you sure? I've had it for a long time. You may want to keep it with me for a while longer. We were married for thirty years."

"I need it."

"For what?"

"That's none of your concern anymore."

"C'mon, Woman, I know you better than that."

I run my fingers through his thinning hair. "Will you ever go gray?" Silence. I take his face in my hands. His skin is not smooth, but I don't mind. I chuckle at his crooked nose, which is never fixed properly after a mishap in an intermural football game at the academy. I want to kiss his full lips.

"You missed so much choosing not to kiss me."

Silence. I take note of his small ears while I allow myself to lean in just below his right ear and take in his essence one more time. I stroke the nape of his neck and move to kiss it ever so softly, barely making contact.

"I'll find a new ride."

He says, "Will you?"

"In time, yes." As I look in his eyes, I remember the day we met and our brief courtship before we married, our wedding day filled with promise and excitement, my pride for him and his service to our country, our children and tapestry.

"Not anymore," I say as I remove my hands from his face. "The woman you knew is in the light now." I reach into his abdomen tenderly then harvest it, a beautiful ball of white light with a tinge of blue. I drink it up. I see the disbelief and resignation in his eyes.

"It's your turn," I instruct. "Take your energy from me." He sits up before he reaches into me, but he then hesitates. "You don't want me to do this, Woman. There's no going back."

"Take your energy from me now. I don't want it. I don't want you."

He reaches, takes hold, pulls it out and tucks it under his shirt. We stare at each other one last time, no words, no smiles, nothing. We have what belongs to ourselves. No words, no smiles, just sadness. I am compelled to hug him, hoping that maybe this final time we are together he will hug back, but he does not, and though disappointed, I understand it is not me. I run my hands down his arms, to his hands, which I hold, then squeeze.

At the sink, I turn back to the family room, and as his image fades out, I bring my hands to heart center and bow.

"The light in me honors the light in you."

He gives me a side look, one that conveys an understanding that we are no more, something he has known much longer than I; he allows this moment to be, and I am grateful to him for his graciousness.

He is gone and in his place is Grief; she is somber and still. We gaze at each other.

"I didn't give you the attention you deserve. It was easier to let Anger in, so much easier, and it took me a long while to find the courage to face me, but now that I have, I understand you are here to help." Grief lowers her gaze and reaches out, and when I let her in, she takes a gentle hold.

I cry while I mourn the losses in my life, but I grieve mostly for my marriage, especially as I recognize I have done this, unaware, throughout our marriage. It is a struggle to be awake. Sobbing uncontrollably, I bend over the sink and release while Grief embraces me. Tears come and go, and sometimes are as a deluge like when Daddy died, and I think of him too, and he makes his presence known. I reach for the faucet, turn on the water, adjust it until it is lukewarm, then splash my face with it. My tears combine with the water until I cannot tell one from the other. I collect myself, grab a dish towel and pat my face dry.

Out the window above the sink, I look beyond the feeders, garden, my house, Poquoson and Virginia, to the west and the Black Hills of South Dakota. "Goodbye husband, fair winds and following seas."

I bring my attention back to my garden, still in need of pruning and weeding. "I'm coming, be patient." The feeders are withering on their pole, empty. "I haven't forgotten you either." My body tells me, *This is how it feels to be there.* Its levity keeps me grounded. I am a divine being having a human experience. Clarity is not a burden. It is bliss. *I've got time,* I think. My handbag on my shoulder, I put on my Birkenstocks and go to the Birds Unlimited for seed.

18
Silver Anniversary

"I can look in the mirror."

Sharon smiles. "How do you feel?"

"Lighter, but something still isn't right."

"And him?"

"I let him go."

"Let's get to the table."

As she works magic with her hands, I'm unsettled but I keep still. Sharon continues, aware of my uneasiness. "What's on your mind?" she says as she makes swirls on my chest.

"I don't know."

"Look within, tell me what you see."

"It's Daddy… I see Daddy."

"And…"

"He's dead, and I see me in the corner sobbing, my eyes are smashed up in my knees and my head shakes from side to side."

"What else?"

"I don't know."

"Don't be frightened, let it play out."

"There are the men at the top of the stairs with him, and here they come down the stairs."

"Keep going."

"I can't stand it. I scream at them in my head; I fall down on the rug and burn my scraped knees; I run behind the server."

Silence.

"Oh, no!" I'm startled.

"What is it?" Sharon pauses.

"I left, a part of me left with him; I see me go out the door. How did I do this? What did I do?"

"His death was traumatic, and you responded as best you could."

"But I'm here. I didn't leave, yet I did, and it was real; it was very real."

"It's a soul fragment, and we can get it back."

"Now?"

"Yes."

I breathe deep and reposition myself. It takes a moment, but I can clear my head to let the music in. Its melody undulates throughout my mind allowing me to relax, to be at peace, to move on from all this including Daddy's death. Sharon resumes her work. It's as if she is frantic. Her hands first make swirls and then she rakes my chest, repeatedly. She is beckoning me to go back to my childhood home to find me and bring her back, and I do with Daddy's help.

I have pieces of our time together, each labeled in the recesses of my mind… pristine, forever frozen, fifty years old. Do I dare revisit what is left after so much loss, longing, and loneliness? You have been gone so long; you would be gone by now. Maybe not. I cannot bear to see us through my middle-aged, farsighted, somewhat jaded eyes. Youthful eyes are forgiving, seeing what we need, though sometimes obscured, they see no consequence. I saw you through them for eight years, and I see you now, but I am grown.

"What do you see, Daughter?"

"You in the distance, standing tall, looking at me, smiling. I know, I *know*. Too much. I think too much; I can't let them be. Always poking, probing, prodding my thoughts along, not trusting… What did you say, Dad?"

"Unsettled?"

"You chose your life path, a short walk, one I walked along with you for a bit."

"I know."

"Our path was filled with colorful flowers until the blight, and then it was barren, a desert without an oasis."

"What else bothers you?"

"Choices, the choices I made without your guidance. The ones I was left to make on my own, and I wasn't good at it. I was alone in my marriage, perpetuating the pattern of my life after you left."

"It's time for a second chance, Daughter."

"What do you mean?"

"New opportunities to be who you are, not who you've been."

"I hope so."

"Do you understand what happened with me?"

"We make our choices about how we want to live on this planet. You chose to leave early, and I chose to be with you."

"Do you know why you chose to be with me?"

"Not yet. I'm not sure about a lot of things except I don't need to be afraid."

"Look back."

"It's difficult."

"It's necessary."

"Brave Girl?"

"Yes."

"Through her eyes?"

"Through her eyes."

Silence.

"Where are you, Brave Girl?"

"In the family room, Daddy, by the chair that is brown and black striped. You know I'm there and move your right hand just enough to fold one corner of the paper. Your dark brown eyes find me. No words. It's easy with us, so I come to you. I climb in and curl up to you. You read, and I look at pictures, just being. I drift off to sleep, your heartbeat rocks me, and I dream we live in a castle behind a wall made of newspaper."

"What else?"

"You teach me. You say, Hold the ball against your chest, cradle it tightly with both arms… Go! I run. My hair is in my eyes and mouth, my balance is not good. The ball falls, so do I, and my head lays low. Did I please you? Am I good at it like you?"

"And?"

"Let's try again, you say. Get behind me, to the left side, girl, over there. Get your arms ready, and when I say three, come to me. I will put the football here. Don't think too much. Trap the ball and run to the patio. Got it?"

"Got it, Daddy."

"One, two, three!"

"I run, you place the football on my chest, I hold it as hard as I can… touchdown!"

"That's more like it, you say. I see the smile on your face."

Silence.

"What's wrong?"

"You're not happy with me. Are you playing? I can't remember, Daddy."

"You're mouthy."

"I run to my bedroom. You are behind me. I feel you and I'm sad, and I almost fall on my way up the stairs. I slam the door shut, dive under the bed, kind of like in a pool. It hurts to lie on my stomach. The door creaks. *Sorry,* I say inside. I tuck my arms under my chest, close my eyes hard, and my face presses into the rug. The bed spread drapes to the floor. *Maybe you'll go away.*

"You come slow, my heart throbs. I count the beats, shiver, squinch into a ball. *Please don't be mad at me, please!* Your belt is loud. You lift the spread and look at me. I go limp, turn my head, open my eyes and say, 'Are you mad, Daddy?'"

Silence.

"You smile, let go of the spread, stand up and put your belt away. Under the bed, I'm not sure what happened, but I'm not cold anymore."

"What is it, Brave Girl?"

"I don't want to look anymore, Daddy."

"What about trips to Boston? Baseball and football games? Vacations to the beach? Suppertime? You laugh at my jokes, and I sing silly rhymes you want to hear."

"I want you, not memories."

"Don't cry."

"I want my Daddy."

"Do you see, Daughter?"

"I do."

"It's time."

"For what?"

"For you two to come together."

"I don't want to go there, Dad."

"Are you afraid?"

"I don't know what I am."

"There is nothing to fear."

"Where are you Brave Girl?"

"Behind the server, Daddy."

"What are you doing?"

"I hear them. I hear the men who come to the house and take you away… No! Don't take my father, please!"

"I'm here."

"No! You're gone forever!"

"I'm here."

"The front door opens, Daddy, there's the loud breathing as they carry you away!"

"Do you see her, Daughter?"

"Yes."

"Do you see what she is doing?"

"Crying. Wailing."

"What else do you see?"

"A piece of her goes out the front door with you."

"You need to get that piece back to her."

"How am I supposed to do that?"

"Welcome her back home. She will be become whole again. You will belong to each other."

"We've been separated forever. What do we have in common?"

"Me."

"I don't see you as she does."

"Would you like to?"

"Would it matter?"

"What matters is wholeness, having something to share. Bring her home."

Silence.

"Do you trust me, Daughter?"

"Yes."

"Then you have to do this."

I'm looking at her, crying, rocking back and forth, inconsolable.

"Don't leave, Daddy! Don't leave me here alone!" Her image becomes stronger, clearer, as she repeats the mantra, "Don't leave me, don't leave me, don't leave me!" Her eyes are red, swollen, and her face is very wet, her hair is sticking to it. She buries her head in her knees, wraps her arms around them and sits. Her uneven breaths jerk her body back and forth. She is defeated. She is broken. With tears welling up in my eyes, I respond.

"It's me, Daughter."

"Don't leave me, don't leave me."

"I won't leave you, come to me." I reach for her. "Come here!" She raises her head, clears the hair from her eyes and looks. "Come! I won't leave you!" She hesitates, retreats into herself and covers her head with her arms. "Please honey, please Brave Girl, come home." She looks again, wipes the hair from her face and reaches back. Our fingers touch, and her light comes into mine.

"Thank you, Dad."

"How do you feel?"

"Spent."

"Whole?"

"On my way."

"And settled?"

"We'll see."

"How is she?"

"Taking it all in."

"What now?"

"What do you mean?"

"Plans?"

"Trying to live in the moment, the eternal now."

"It's where I am."

"Can we visit again?"

"Just think of me."

"Just hang around."

"I do."

"Oh?"

"Your awareness connects us like this."

The Tibetan bells chime. "Take a deep breath and come back to this place, space and time." I hear running water which means my session is over. I sit up, haphazardly move my hair from my face, get down and walk to the recliner. I tie my hair back while Sharon jots down notes.

"Well," she says, laughing. "I can see something happened."

"She's with me."

"And..."

"It feels like everything is right with me."

"Of course it does, the two of you are together again."

"Is this why I've felt incomplete, like I've had a hole in me."

"Could be. Trauma can cause a host of issues; soul fragmentation is one of them."

"It's been fifty years, Sharon, since he died. Fifty years this week and just now, my grieving is over."

"Amen."

19
Living

My hiatus from the life I led in Poquoson is dubbed "Mom's walkabout" by my eldest. With my energy restored, my marriage reconciled, my truth defined, I begin the walk again. After the sale of my family's home in February 2018, I go north for a month while I wait for the lease to expire on my rental property in Yorktown. It has been three years since the split, and it is time to move on to a new chapter, and eventually begin a new adventure, but first, I transition at The Dog House. I feel that it is an auspicious time; I can exhale.

The Dog House is a 700-square foot retreat situated on a well maintained fifty-two-acre estate named Oak Hall in Gloucester County. The main house complements the banks of the North River. She is splendid in design and not ostentatious: a classic Greek Revival Manor built at the turn of the 20th century, she is painted a cheerful yellow, and her black shutters and white trim immediately calm me. The chimneys stand very tall and straight, a testament to the home's enduring presence in the pastoral setting. I think the name of the estate is peculiar since there are only a few grand oaks on the property in front of the main entrance, but I learn many were lost during Hurricane Isabel. I can only imagine the grandeur these trees, perhaps saplings during the American Revolution, projected, and I lament their demise and feel for those trees still standing, wondering how they adapted to the loss.

It is Good Friday. A bald eagle is perched atop one of the trees, surveying its domain and waiting for the opportunity to hunt or scavenge on the river. It cocks its head from side to side, then looks up and down and listens. It is a bird of prey, impressive, its reputation well earned, and as I study him, it is clear why Benjamin Franklin thought it was an appropriate symbol for our country. This creature owns its territory without apology. It comes into sight as I write, and it is magnificent. Its head and tail feathers are bright white, and I see its yellow nib and claws. I get up from my desk to sit on a club chair at the picture window. I wait.

It circles high above the river in the blue sky sparsely populated with cumulus clouds that conjure an image of an exploded box of extra-large cotton balls glued to the sky. I think about Mother's beauty supplies and the years spent lying on my back looking up at the clouds, and I laugh that I still see them with childlike perception. The eagle leans forward and lowers its head toward the water before it descends; its wings expand, they guide and balance it as it swoops down quickly with the air current, spreads its tail feathers and talons and snatches the water. "Missed," I say. I watch it climb back up to make another approach and then another, and though its efforts are unsuccessful, they are remarkable, and it retreats to the loblolly pines on the banks of the boat basin.

Other fauna grace the river: mallards, loons, grebes, egrets and sea gulls. Deer, rabbits, turkeys and a variety of songbirds, whose melodies nearly deafen me in the mornings and late afternoons, are frequent visitors.

The house is well maintained, and though the lawn is not pristine, the green is mowed regularly and edged. The shrubbery is impressive: quince as tall as twelve feet and just as wide, Camellias, at least nine feet, a Viburnum to the right of the retreat has a diameter of at least ten feet, and Edgeworthian, one of my favorite spring bloomers, is over four feet tall. Its delicate clusters of white flowers open beneath my picture window throughout the month I stay at The Dog House, and their scent is pleasing, relaxing like a cup of chamomile tea. There are redbuds, magnolias, azaleas, dogwoods and hydrangeas. The estate has an extensive daylily garden I do not see bloom, but I imagine it is a spectacular display of color at the height of its season as a fireworks finale.

Although the name "Dog House" implies an inferior residence, it is not. On the contrary, it is in keeping with the manor: genteel, comfortable, a country home in miniature. I enter its presence through French doors. Directly in front of me is a picture window overlooking the North River, about 100 yards away. A leather couch sits beside the window with two club chairs and a coffee table. On the coffee table are a couple of books of interest, a pair of binoculars, and a candle. To my left is a queen size sleigh bed made with plush linens and decorated with shams, throw pillows, and an overstuffed comforter. I organize my clothes in an antique dresser. To my right is an antique armoire I use for work clothes and the kitchenette, which includes a coffee maker, toaster oven, refrigerator, and microwave. To the right of it is the bathroom, a crisp-looking space decorated with white tile and a modern pedestal sink and shower. The Dog House is awash with reds, blues, browns and golden tones.

Behind the bed are stocked bookshelves I peruse one evening. I find a couple of first edition children's books I assume belong to the master of the manor. He died many years ago, but his wife continues to care for the estate. His portrait hangs on the wall directly to the right in the entrance to the house. He was a tall, attractive man, distinguished, and as the painting illustrates, devoted to golden retrievers. Two pose with him. His love for them is present throughout the retreat in wall hangings, the bed linen and decorative pillows. The Dog House is a shrine to goldens; it is their space. I am their guest.

I watch the sun come out from behind a cloud and decide to go for a walk along the riverfront. I close my laptop, put on my fall jacket, put my hair up and stroll to the Adirondack chairs facing the river. Before I get to the river's edge the sun is covered again, but when I reach it, the billowy cloud moves on and the sun shines. I swipe some leaves off of a chair and sit.

All I hear is the water as it moves downriver. The air is wet and chilled, and I am not sure I will stay. A cool breeze sends chills up my spine, but I settle in, picking my legs up and tucking them underneath myself crisscrossed. My time in Gloucester is short term and my desire to experience this precious retreat and its natural surroundings supersedes my desire for warm temperatures. As a seagull passes by, it interrupts the churning of the water when it looks at me and squawks. I look up to it. "I don't have anything to feed you." It squawks again and turns its attention upriver. I turn my attention inward and I allow the river's melody to help me transition. I close my eyes.

Thank you for my life. Thank you for my family and those in my life who love me. What an adventure it has been. From the depths of sorrow, confusion and anger, I am here. Peace is with me; she is my friend. There are no obstacles, only opportunities to love, to understand and enjoy. I am one with all creation. I open my eyes and look across the river to the houses there. I spy a large brick house with three dormers. It reminds me of mine.

She sells in ten days. In our more than two years together, I have paid attention to her aches and groans, learning her wants and needs. She needs extensive work, but she is worth it since she gives me years of herself, providing me the space to raise my family, the ground to garden and a community to live in.

I replace the dilapidated side door to the garage and the front door first. I choose black doors to complement the celadon vinyl siding and forest green shudders. I buy a storm door that allows crisp air to flow through the house in the early spring and fall. I hang an awning above the side door to the garage that shelters me from the rain. It is black with white piping trim. I replace all six outdoor light fixtures and these make a tremendous difference on the house's appearance. It is as though she is given a pair of pearl earrings and matching necklace. She is instantly classic, yet modern. A new garage door is put in and the trim work around it is wrapped in PVC molding to prevent future rotting. I install a garage door opener and replace the gutters, and she breathes a sigh of relief when the rain no longer leaks through the barriers. She is bathed with a power wash and her siding glistens, rejuvenated. All the rotted wood is replaced, and after I paint the trim, she looks ten years younger. I repair the chimney, too, all its broken bricks fixed, and its crevices filled; she appears stronger and taller once this work is finished.

The foyer gets a facelift with fresh paint for the walls and trim. Carpet is replaced. All her systems have check-ups and any irregularities are addressed and repaired. Her windows are cleaned the week of her debut on the market, and the day I put her up for sale she is mine entirely, and I realize we are kindred spirits too. We are a bit out of sorts, but we have life flowing through us. What we need is support, understanding and love, and we are fortunate because we get all these.

I sell her to a family I know will appreciate her as I have through the years, and she deserves a family, not a single woman whose interest in homemaking is replaced with other desires. I pull out of her driveway for the last time at 6 a.m., shift into gear and drive. Just beyond the mailbox, though, something compels me to stop. I unbuckle my seatbelt and turn around, lifting myself off the seat just enough to wrap my right arm around the back of the driver's seat and get a good look at what is no longer mine. She is dressed up and ready to welcome her new family, and I am filled with pride because she is beautiful.

Against her foundation, the tete-a-tete daffodils are in bloom. I planted a couple hundred over the years in the front bed; now naturalized there and prosperous, I cannot imagine a more gracious gesture to welcome the new family. Out back the forsythia, also in bloom, border the bronzed colored bricks of the patio, creating a warm space for anyone wishing to dawdle there. Korean spice viburnum, whose fragrant scent welcomes all visitors to the back garden, will bloom in a week or two, and I know I will miss it a lot. The butterfly garden is beginning to reveal itself and I hope the new family will be patient and let it be, at least for the first spring, and maybe they will love it as I do and keep it. Lady Banks' rose is tame, her last pruning done several months prior before the growing season. She is draped over a wrought iron arch I installed several years back. It is unique, a novelty. The climber will give her new owners small white flowers by the end of April, and since I do not have the heart to disrupt her, I leave her and my beloved arch behind. I spy my pawpaw tree at the edge of the butterfly garden, and I regret I do not have the strength to dig him up. He and the zebra swallowtail are one of the summer highlights in my garden. The latter lays her eggs on the tree, one egg per leaf, and once the eggs hatch, the caterpillars' only source of food are the young pawpaw leaves. The variety of pawpaw in my region only grows here, so the two have evolved together. I hope to find one at The Living Museum's annual plant sale to have in my new garden by the river.

It is difficult to perceive, but I swear I see a little boy with an uncanny resemblance to my son to the left of the pawpaw tree in front of the arch that leads to the butterfly garden. I lean forward and squint. It is him! He is six, maybe seven years old. He has a small model of a navy fighter plane in his right hand, and it is in a death spiral and headed for my terra cotta pot. It crashes there and he buries it unceremoniously, covering it with dirt and then leaving it there without parting words or even a salute. *How you loved it when I found it, brushed it off and gave it back to you. This was our time in the garden.*

From behind me comes the sound of leather on leather, so I turn around a bit more, tighten my hold on the driver's seat and see my girls playing catch on the front lawn. "Not so hard, Sis," and her reply, "You can catch it." *I pray you two stay close as the years unwind. I pray the three of you love each other as I have loved you.* An upswell of emotion comes over me, but it is not melancholy; it is satisfaction. I shift into gear again and my companion Peace, a beautiful multi-colored orb, is with me up front in the passenger seat. She and I drive away in the quiet of predawn.

Good Friday is a day of fasting and reflection on the crucifixion of Christ. In another time, I fasted and went to Mass, but in this time, I am in Gloucester County, and I do not fast or go to Mass, but I think about The Christ, Logos and Teacher, nonetheless. The Christ came to usher in a new age, a time for us to reconcile our humanity with our divinity, a time to forgive and love. I am comfortable with Him even though our relationship has changed. I am no longer a child afraid of judgment and filled with guilt. I am a child filled with love, and although I am His child, so to speak, I am also His friend. In years past, Good Friday was heavy and solemn, but Good Friday now is light and hopeful. It occurs to me as I ruminate in the quiet of nature's noise that last year, on Good Friday, a blessing was bestowed, a new beginning, a fresh start for my family and me. She weighed seven pounds one ounce, and she had dark hair and olive colored skin. Her name: Lilian Beth.

I get up and go back to the cottage to retrieve the words I had written to her. They are stored on my laptop. I pick it up and hurry back outside to the river's edge. As I sit down, a mother and her ducklings swim into the boat basin in a tidy row, spaced apart with equal measure and I recall the children's book, *Make Way for Ducklings*. The Boston Public Garden immortalized the story with a bronze statue of the mother and her brood, and I watched children play on and around it when I hung out there in my early twenties. The mallard and her babies swim toward shore at the back of the basin while the word document opens. I adjust the screen to deflect glare from the sun before I read.

My Dearest,

I hate flying, I really do. I'm a landlubber and your Lolo loves the earth. She loves to dig in it and to inhale the aroma of it, especially healthy soil. She loves to plant flowers, shrubs, trees, food, anything that will grow and give back to her. I love being on the water too, though. The salt spray on my face cleanses my skin and the sound of water as it washes ashore or up against a boat brings Peace, and she heals. With trepidation, I board an American Airlines flight to be with you, my first grandchild.

I have no idea how to respond to your beauty, and I wonder what my role needs to be. My desire is to serve you, to love you authentically and to model what a successful and healthy woman looks like. I wonder if you'll ask me one day why your Pop Pop and I aren't married anymore, and I think about this thirty thousand feet above you. I might as well tell you now since I am able to communicate on paper, I think, better than face to face when it comes to this kind of thing.

Your Pop Pop and I were married for thirty years. We had promise; both of us were (and still are) intelligent people. I looked forward to marriage. To me, he was bigger than life, and I was very happy to marry him at twenty-four. Pop Pop did for me as best he could. He knew I'd take care of him, your mother, aunt and uncle and our life while he focused on supporting us and his naval career. We suffered in our personal life though, and I hoped we could bridge the gap between us. Unfortunately, the gap widened until it became too difficult to close. Our journey together ended. He chose another path and I eventually did too. Before we parted, I thought about how our split would impact you, your siblings, and cousins, but it became clear you deserved healthy adults in your life. I couldn't be healthy unless I was on my own; being alone was my only recourse in the end, and as I write this, I am still saddened by the loss of my marriage. I am sorry I couldn't give you the gift of an intact family, but I do love you very much, and I give you all I have.

What a landing! Stellar! Now, I can focus on you, only you! Your father comes to pick me up at the terminal. It is overcast and a bit nippy, and I am disappointed the weather isn't better, at least warmer and sunny.

I still don't know Daddy very well, but I'd like to understand the man and the father, and I'm sure I will as the years unfold. We visit on the ride to your house and he points out various places along the way. Texas goes on and on! I'm used to a peninsula, which means I have water all around me. You have lots of land and no water. Your mommy doesn't care for Tidewater, but I like it there and for now it is home.

You are breathtaking. These words loop in my mind as I hold you for the first time. You remind me of your mother, but I see you, my dearest, with your blue eyes, your puffy cheeks, your long slender fingers, little ears and head of hair. You stretch like a yogini, completely and with purpose from the top of your head all the way to your feet, even your toes are stretched out. You sleep with character, one arm wrapped around my shoulder, the other tucked underneath your chin. You are eight days old and you are grand, confident already, and I cannot help but think I am going to enjoy the little girl you will be in a short time, running around, commanding your stuffies and dollies, all the while the pride and joy of the grownups in your life.

We take our first nap together. I do not plan this, it just happens naturally. You are on my chest, lying over my heart. Can you hear it beating? Does it soothe you and keep you feeling safe? Your tiny legs are tucked up under you, like a tree frog, and your right arm rests on my shoulder while your left arm leans up against your body. I rest my head on the arm of the sofa and my legs are bent. It is warm so we are not covered.

When you are asleep, your face grimaces, your lips pucker and you flinch, but you are at ease, and I bathe you in white light and beckon your guardians to stay near. I will teach you to listen to them.

I take long, deep, purposeful breaths for you, and the rise and fall of my chest lulls you while you rest and keeps me focused on us and the moment we share. You do not stir, not even a bit. You are secure, my gentle embrace keeps you safe. We are one, and I savor our time alone and allow myself to be lullabied by you. Sublime is the word to describe the ensuing hour.

xox

I missed her birth, but I witness the birth of Jake, my daughter's son, who is born about a year later. The plan was for her to be induced on March 8, in the evening, if she didn't begin labor naturally. She is a brave woman whose positive attitude impresses me, but I know she is concerned, not so much for the baby but for herself because she wants to deliver naturally. We speak on the phone daily.

"How are you feeling, honey?"

"Good, Mommy."

"Any pangs?"

"No."

"Are you visualizing?"

"I am, and I called my cousin. She's visualizing too, and we've bathed him in light. It'll be all right, honey. You can visualize too, see the baby on the bullseye."

"Keep doing it, Mommy."

"I will, honey."

"I'm on all fours trying to move him. I've always seen myself delivering naturally. I can't believe it might not happen."

"See what you want to see and work toward it."

"It's not like me to not listen to the doctor. I felt badly about it, but we want to let it go if we can until we can't."

"I support you."

"I'll call you when I get to the hospital tomorrow night."

"Okay, I love you."

"Love you too."

I am in the tub before dawn on Thursday, March 8 when I hear the ding from my cell phone. I pick it up off the tile floor. "We'll know in an hour if we're staying," the text says, with a picture of her in a hospital bed. It is almost 5:00a.m.

"What? I thought you were going to the hospital this evening?" I text back.

"She went into labor last night. She lost her plug."

My eyes fill with water. "Let me know." I put the phone down. Crying and praising the heavens, I get dressed, pack an overnight bag and put in for a leave of absence.

He texts at 5:30. "We're staying, she's at four centimeters."

"I'm on my way."

I listen to uplifting music while I drive and play it loudly and sing along on Interstates 64, 295, 95, and 85. Once on Route 1, I speed and crank it up more. I think about her, about all my children, actually, and about the miracle of life and its ability to transform; its drive to move forward, sometimes dragging us along because we cannot keep up. At this juncture, I am grateful for it; even though I can keep up with it, I stumble quite often, I get stuck. "Thank you," I say out loud. "Thank you for moving forward and taking me with you."

I hurry into my daughter's room; she is on all fours and at nine centimeters. "I'm going to push soon Mommy." I take my jacket off and lay it and my briefcase on the lounge chair near her bed. Although I am hesitant to be with her while she delivers, feeling she and her husband should experience the birth of their child alone, I can tell from their expressions that they want to share the birth of their son, my grandson, with me. They know better than I their birthing experience is mine too. I wash my hands, roll up my sleeves and go to my daughter's bedside.

Nurse Brittany says, "Are we ready to have a baby?"

"Ready," she says.

"Okay, can you get back into the bed, onto your side? I think this will help the baby get into position." Brittany and my son-in-law help my daughter while she maneuvers herself into position. I ready myself to be her doula.

"Let's give a good push: one, two, three, deep breath, hold it, now bear down and push," says Brittany. I take her hand. "Push from below, not with your face, good, that's it," I say.

"Good push," says Brittany.

I brush her hair back from her face while she positions herself for another push. She grabs my hand; her grip is tight, and I channel my energy and strength to her.

"Deep breath, hold it, now push, keep pushing," says Brittany.

"Keep it up, bear down honey, not in the face, good," I say.

"I see the head." says Brittany.

My son-in-law looks. "He has hair!"

"A couple more pushes and he'll be ready to be born," Brittany observes.

She repositions herself again, takes my hand, and inhales. "Push now, keep going," Brittany coaches.

"Bear down honey, good girl, beautiful work," I say.

"The doctor will be here in just a minute." Brittany leaves the room.

"You were awesome, honey."

"Thanks, Mommy. Does he have a lot of hair?"

He says, "It's hard to tell, but he has it."

"Good," she says.

The doctor comes in, along with the birthing team, and they get ready by preparing the neonatal station and by putting on birthing scrubs. They put her legs into stirrups while the ceiling opens and a birthing lamp comes down for the doctor. "Whoa," I say, "Hydraulics! I've never seen such stuff before." I look at several computer monitors to the right of her bed, each programmed to measure something: the baby's heartbeat, my daughter's heart rate and contractions.

"I am amazed. I didn't have all this when I had you."

"High tech babies," she comments. "Thank a STEM major." My chemist and her biologist laughed.

"Very funny," the writer says. "Remember, it's the artists who keep you sane through their music, images, and words. STEM isn't everything." We chuckle.

"Let's have a baby," the doctor says.

My son-in-law stands to my daughter's left and takes hold of her left thigh. I stand at her head and support her while she wraps her arms around both the backs of her thighs, inhales deeply, and pushes.

"Good push," the doctor says. "Keep pushing! Good! Keep going, a little longer... that's it! Inhale... hold it and push! Push, push again! Here we go, push! Keep pushing, he's coming, excellent! One more time, inhale, now bear down and push! Push! Here he comes!" And my grandson is here just like that! "Well done my love, well done... four and a half pushes," I say.

My daughter sinks back into the bed and closes her eyes. I go to the sofa beneath the window to sit down. The baby is wrapped up in his umbilical cord, and after his father cuts it, I watch the doctor free him from it ever so gently.

"Your cord goes on and on," the doctor says. After she delivers the placenta, the doctor pulls the remainder of it from her body. *It's got to be six feet long,* I think as I watch. While the doctor cleans her, I turn my attention to the nurses with my grandson. They handle him with such ease, working together, flipping him over and back again while one cleans and another diapers him. I find myself entranced with his tiny feet and toes.

"Look at his toes! He can spread them apart so far!" I comment as I stand over him.

"I can too," my son-in-law says as he takes off one of his shoes, sock, and splays his toes. "He's mine!"

"Yes, he is!" We laugh.

"What's so funny?" she asks from across the room.

"He has your husband's toes," I answer.

"I like his toes," she smiles. "I tore, Mommy."

"It's okay, honey. You were marvelous, a natural." I walk over to her.

"Almost finished," the doctor says.

She sutures the last stich, ties it off, then gets up from her stool to clean up. I sit on the lounge chair, halfway between the window and my daughter's bed, and once the area around her is cleaned up and all the equipment is turned off and the lamp retracts back into the ceiling, a nurse brings my children their baby.

She places him on her chest, his face is turned away from me. He wears a pink stocking cap (all births prior to his, seven I think, are boys, so all the blue caps are gone). My son-in-law stands over his wife and child, and my daughter looks to him briefly before they turn their gaze to the precious one in their midst. I see the transformation in both immediately: I have witnessed not only the birth of my grandson but also the birth of a family. *He will be the most gratifying experience of your lives.* I sit back in the lounger; my children study their boy with wonder and gratitude. Their son arrived in his own time.

"Thank you for being here, Mommy."

"Thank you for wanting me, sweetheart."

"Of course we wanted you." She smiles. "Will you stay the weekend?"

"Let's get a picture of the three of you. It'll be your first family photo." They turn to face me, but I say, "No, as you are is much better." As they look back at their son, they fall into the trance, and as I take out my phone and get it ready, a lovely thought prances before me: *There is so much more to come, and I am ready to be present for all of it.*

I snap the picture.

Acknowledgements

Writing is a solitary endeavor, but the business of publishing is a collaborative effort. Thank you Mark Willen, Peter Porosky, Amanda Rooker and Michele Young Stone for your generous time and constructive advice. Your input is in this work. Gratitude is expressed for my editor Jane Handa and my publisher Narielle Living. Your guidance and encouragement has made my first steps into the publishing world a pleasant experience.

About the Author

Laura grew up and was educated in New England; its influence is undeniable, yet Virginia is home, and it is there she enjoys her garden with her beloved kitties, Jefferson and Adams, who both romp among the perennials while she weeds. When not gardening, Laura writes and reads those whose words have stood the test of time. She is humbled by their talent. She can be found at laurafiorentino.com.

CPSIA information can be obtained
at www.ICGtesting.com
Printed in the USA
LVHW090339060321
680568LV00008BA/90